GW01339518

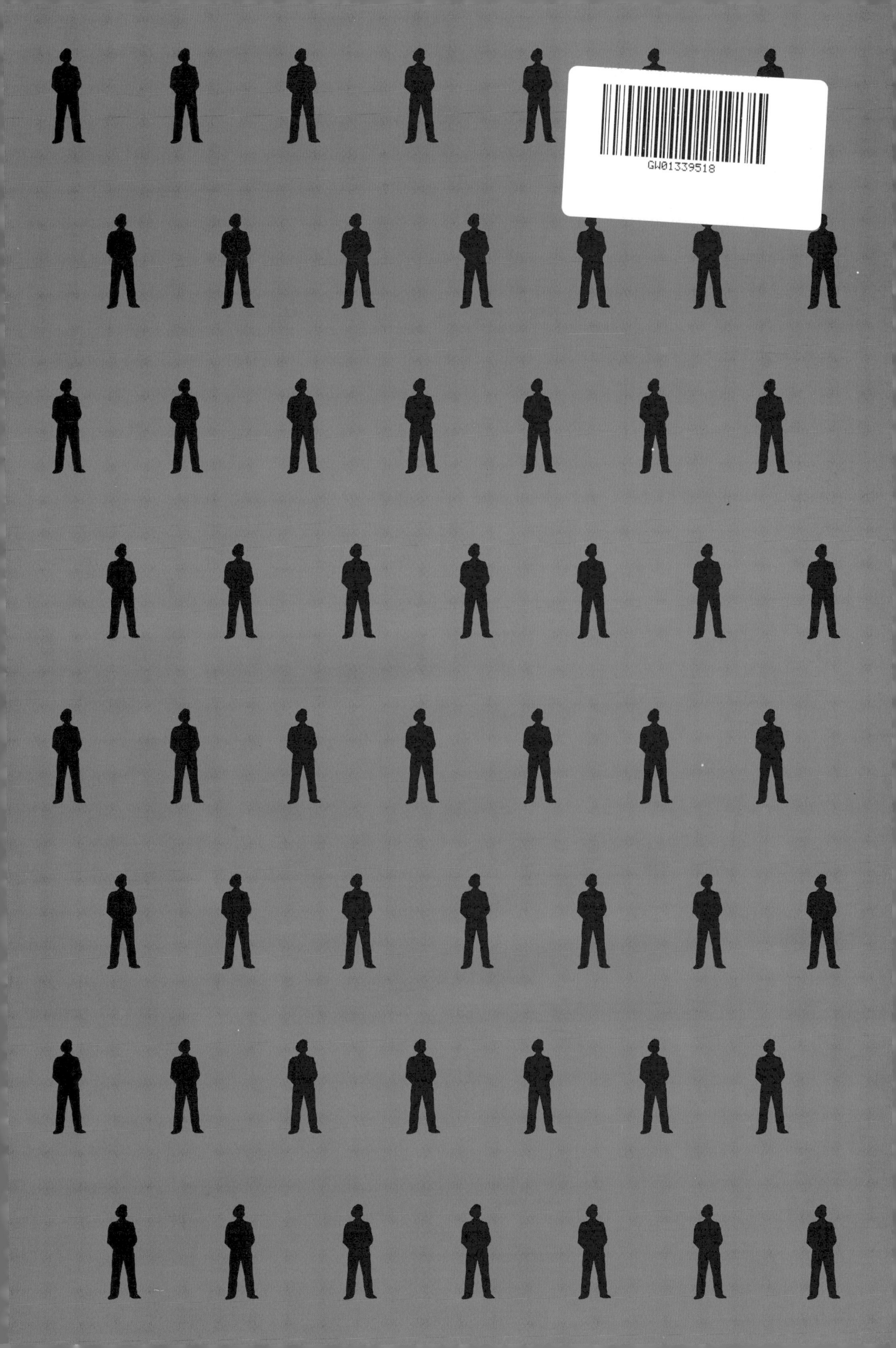

MONTY

CAXTON EDITIONS
AN IMPRINT OF CAXTON PUBLISHING GROUP
20 BLOOMSBURY STREET, LONDON WC1 3QA

© CAXTON EDITIONS, 2001

ALL RIGHTS RESERVED. NO PART OF THIS PUBLICATION MAY BE
REPRODUCED, STORED IN A RETRIEVAL SYSTEM OR TRANSMITTED IN ANY
FORM OR BY ANY MEANS, WITHOUT THE PERMISSION OF
THE COPYRIGHT HOLDER.

ISBN 1 84067 158 0

A COPY OF THE CIP DATA IS AVAILABLE FROM THE
BRITISH LIBRARY UPON REQUEST.

DESIGNED AND PRODUCED FOR CAXTON EDITIONS
BY KEITH POINTING DESIGN CONSULTANCY

REPROGRAPHICS BY GA GRAPHICS
PRINTED AND BOUND IN
SINGAPORE BY APP PRINTING

ACKNOWLEDGMENTS
THE IMPERIAL WAR MUSEUM
DESIGN AND PRODUCTION ASSISTANCE:
MIKI HIRAI AND RIKAKO SUZUKI

COPY EDITOR: SASHA BEHAR

MONTY

A PICTORIAL HISTORY OF HIS SECOND WORLD WAR

KEVIN JONES

CAXTON EDITIONS

MONTY
FIELD MARSHAL
VISCOUNT MONTGOMERY
OF ALAMEIN
1887
KG GCB DSO
1976

CONTENTS

Introduction 7

Montgomery's Early Life and Career 11

Victory at El Alamein 27

From Tunisia to Italy 63

D-Day and the Battle of Normandy 101

From Arnhem to Final Surrender 135

Montgomery as Military Commander 167

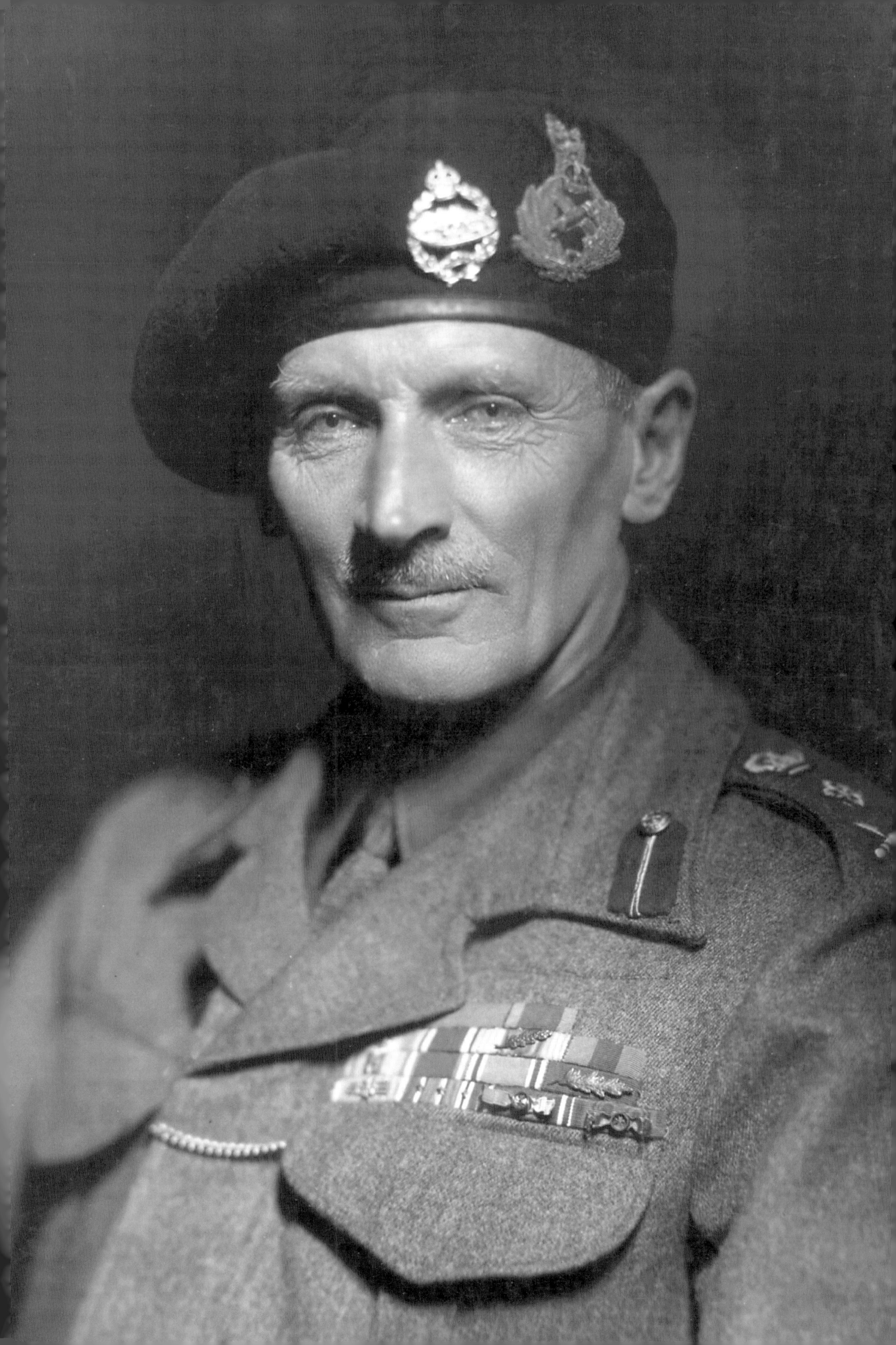

INTRODUCTION

FIELD MARSHAL THE VISCOUNT MONTGOMERY of Alamein was undoubtedly the most famous and influential British general of the Second World War and possibly Britain's most famous military figure since the Duke of Wellington.

He masterminded the first victory over the German Army at El Alamein and went on to play a key role in the campaigns that ended Hitler's domination of Western Europe. He was very much a

LEFT: **Montgomery sits for a formal photographic portrait, 1944.**

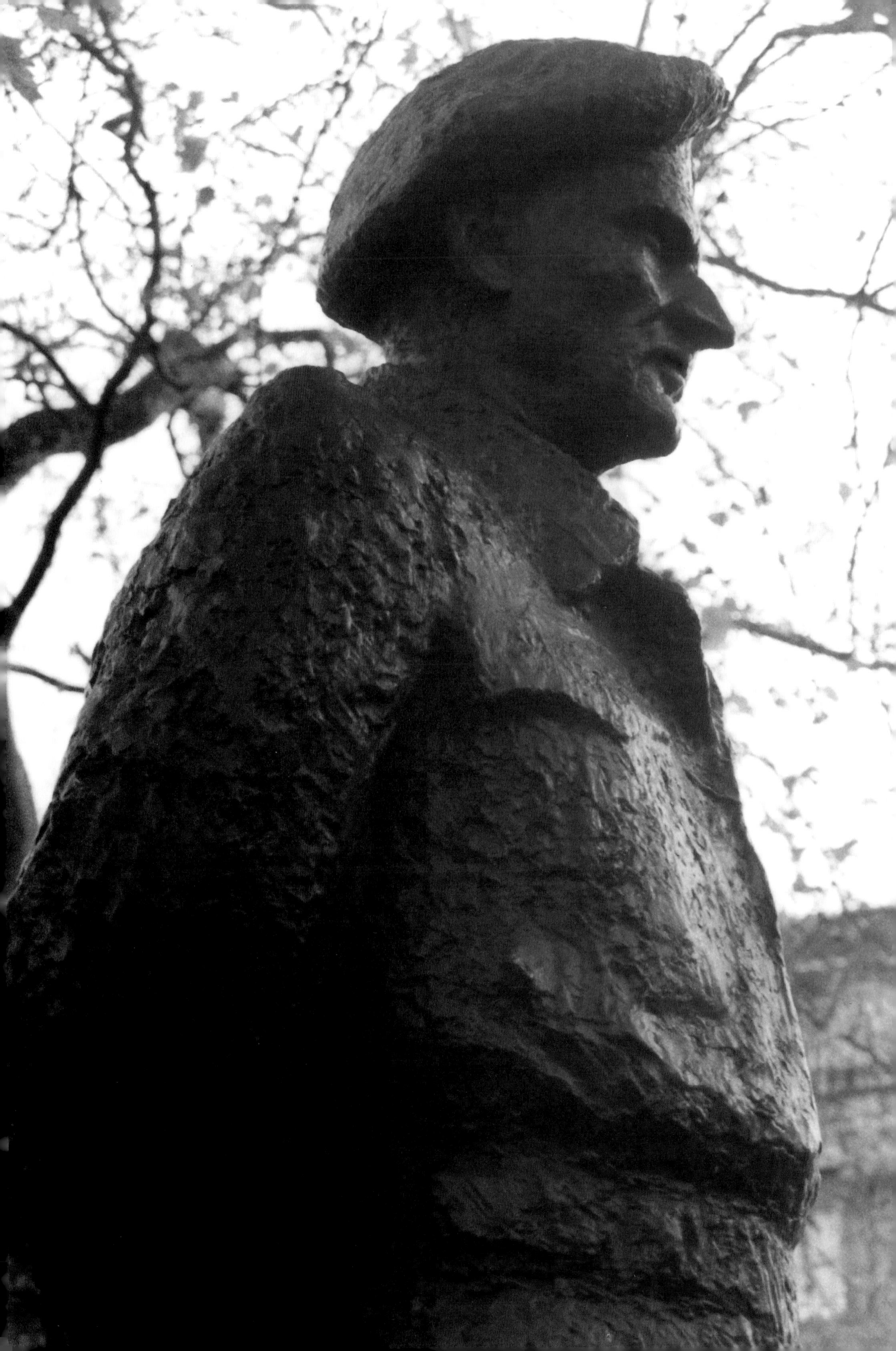

INTRODUCTION

'soldier's general', with the ability to consistently inspire the men under his command. However, his vain self-confidence, that often bordered on arrogance, led Montgomery to treat many of his colleagues and superiors, particularly his American counterparts, with barely concealed contempt. As Winston Churchill once said of him: 'In defeat, unbeatable; in victory, unbearable.'

The shortcomings of Montgomery's personality have done much to tarnish his military reputation during the Second World War, and since then historical opinion has been divided on just how good a military commander he actually was. This book will survey Montgomery's career during the Second World War and then offer an assessment of his military 'genius'.

LEFT: **A statue of Montgomery in characteristic pose, Whitehall, London.**

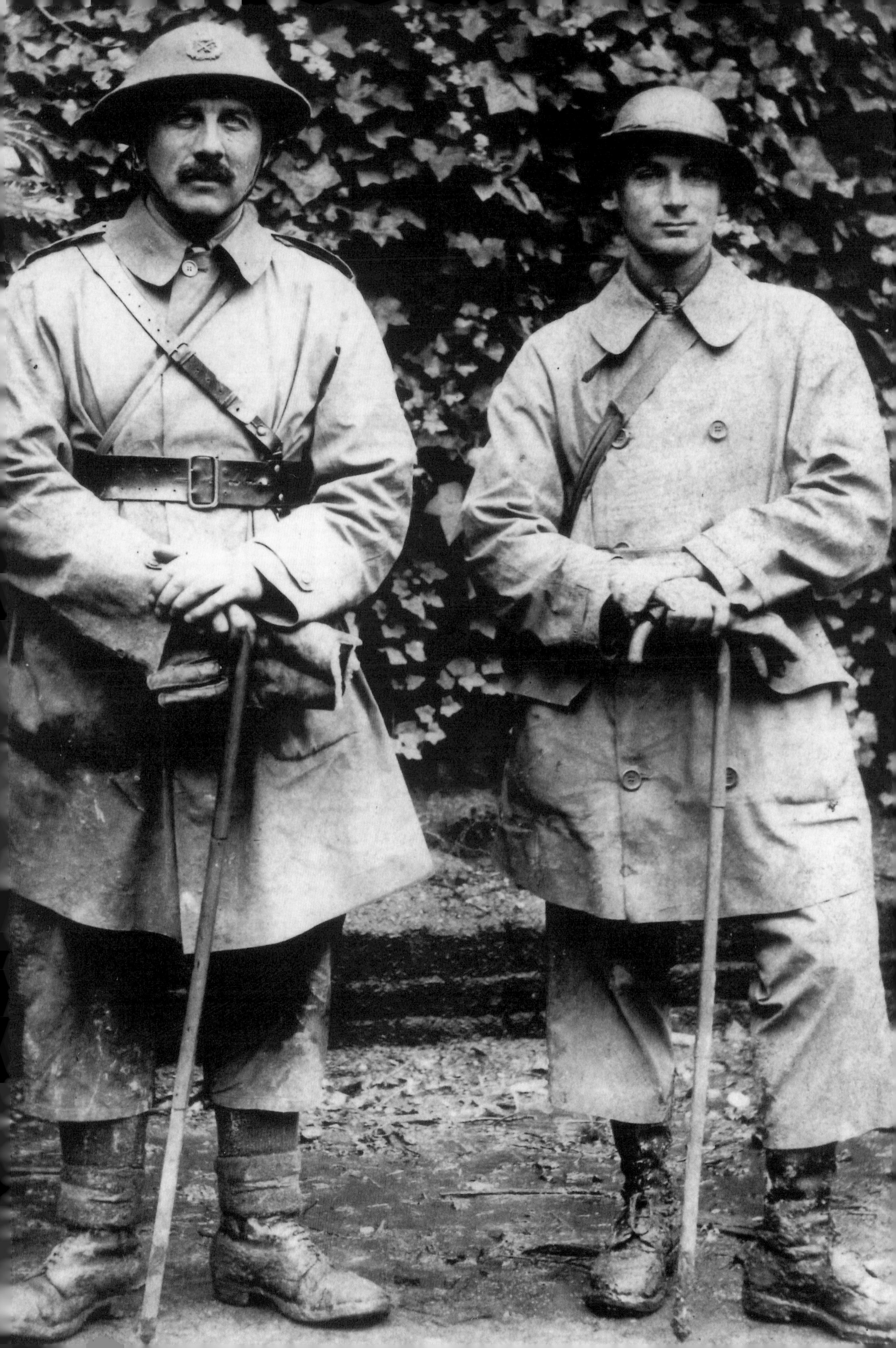

CHAPTER 1

MONTGOMERY'S EARLY LIFE AND CAREER

BERNARD LAW MONTGOMERY was born on 17 November 1887, at Kennington in South London, the fourth child of the Reverend Henry Montgomery and his wife Maud. When Bernard was only two, his family moved to Tasmania where his father had been consecrated Bishop, and the next eleven years had a profound effect on the young Montgomery. With his father away from the family home for long

LEFT: **Captain Bernard Montgomery DSO (on the right of the picture) with a fellow officer of the 104st Infantry Brigade, 35th Division, with which he served from January 1915 until early 1917.**

periods of time, the strong-willed Bernard repeatedly rebelled against his authoritarian mother and he was consequently starved of her affection.

During what he later described as an unhappy childhood, Montgomery became something of a loner, harbouring feelings of rejection that would later affect his ability to achieve close relationships with his contemporaries.

Possibly as a means of escaping his home life, Montgomery decided upon entering St Paul's School in January 1902 as a fourteen year old, to join the Army Class. Despite his parents' opposition, Montgomery persisted and on 30 January 1907, entered the Royal Military College at Sandhurst, having passed the entrance examination ranked 72nd out of 177 cadets. On 19 September 1908, Montgomery finally earned his commission, although he was held back a term and almost expelled for setting fire to the shirt-tails of another cadet, causing severe burns. Certainly Montgomery never smoked and drank only occasionally, but his propensity for violence followed him to his first posting with the 1st Battalion of the Royal Warwickshire Regiment to the North-West Frontier of India at the end of 1908. Here, together with other officers, Montgomery wrecked the Bombay Yacht Club in a drunken melée. However, unlike his colleagues, Montgomery was sober and apparently joined in merely for the enjoyment of it. Nevertheless, he took his profession seriously and upon his return home at the end of 1912, Montgomery was promoted to Assistant-Adjutant of the battalion at the age of only 25.

Upon the outbreak of the First World War in August 1914, Montgomery's battalion was posted to France where, after only three days, he commanded a platoon in an attack on Le Cateau. During the poorly planned assault, Montgomery lost many of his men and went missing himself for several days. Later, on 13 October 1914, during the First Battle of Ypres, Montgomery again led a platoon in a brave attack on the village of Meteren, for which he earned promotion to captain and was awarded the Distinguished Service Order for conspicuous gallantry, an unusually high decoration for a junior officer. During this action, however, Montgomery was all but killed by a sniper's bullet through the lungs and returned to England to recuperate.

Ironically, the severity of his wounds almost certainly ensured his survival throughout the rest of the war, for instead of returning to the front-line, Montgomery thereafter served as a General Staff officer. Returning to France on 12 February 1915 as a Brigade-Major in the

MONTGOMERY'S EARLY LIFE AND CAREER

112th Infantry Brigade, Montgomery subsequently gained valuable experience, at increasingly higher levels of command, of the planning and execution of military operations. By July 1918, he had risen to the temporary rank of Lieutenant-Colonel, and virtual chief of staff, at the headquarters of the 47th Division and ended the war with a reputation for efficient staff work and tough leadership.

Following demobilization, Montgomery returned as a student to the Staff College at Camberley where he became firm friends with fellow student Alan Brooke, a friendship that would develop into the key

OVERLEAF: **The Lille Victory Parade, November 1918, is watched by Lieutenant-Colonel Montgomery, behind whom is Winston Churchill, Minister of Munitions.**

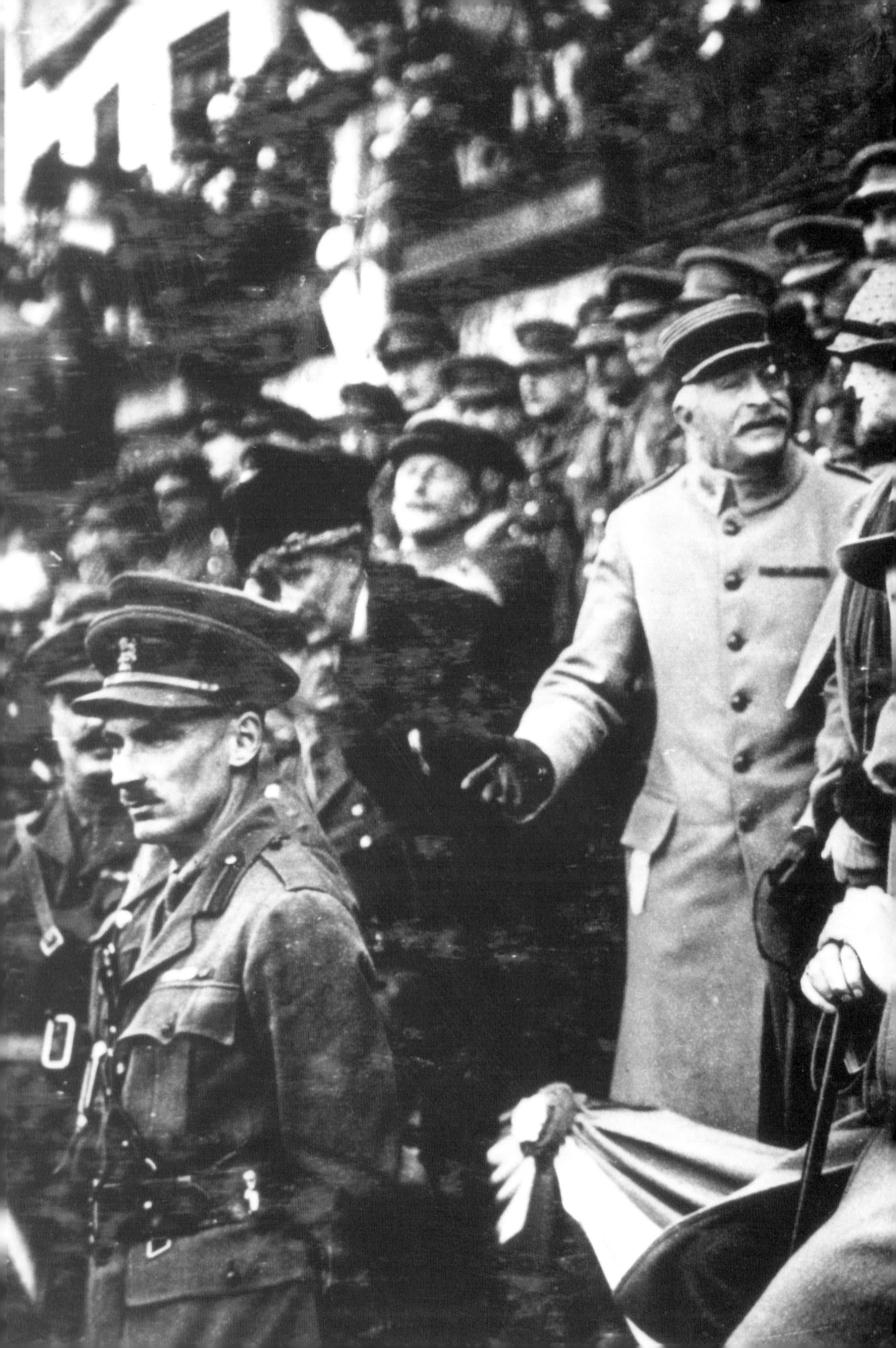

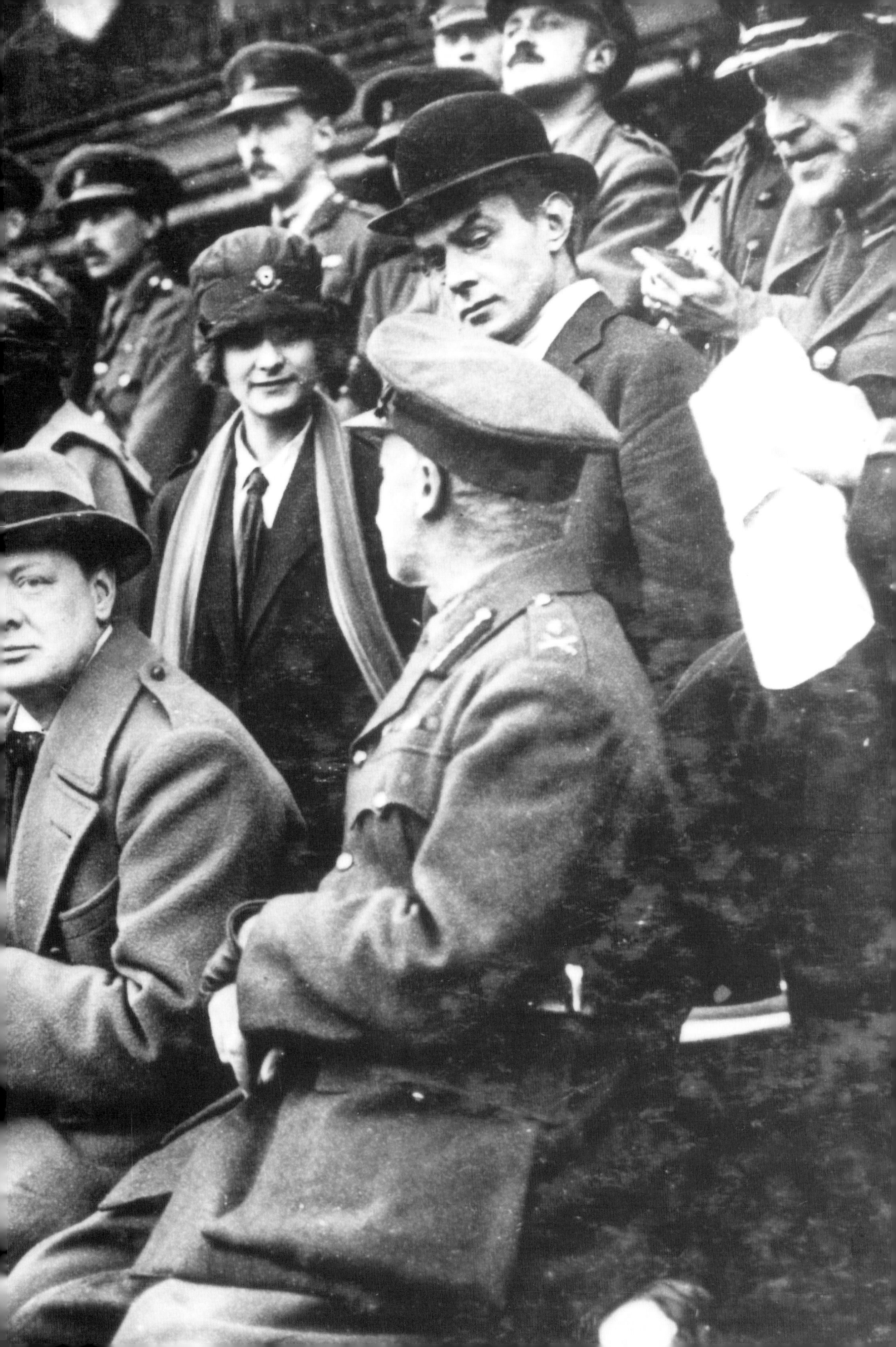

professional relationship of Montgomery's career. After graduation, Montgomery alternated between training appointments and overseas postings. As a training instructor, firstly at Camberley between 1926 and 1929 and then at Quetta Staff College as Chief Instructor, from 1934 to 1937, Montgomery soon found his niche. Actively encouraging his students, but also chiding any laziness, he brought to his teaching both logic and a mastery of detail and learnt himself, much about the art of battlefield command. In between these appointments, Montgomery was posted to Palestine and Egypt as commanding officer of the 1st Battalion Royal Warwicks and following his time at Quetta, was given command of the 9th Infantry Brigade, based at Portsmouth, on 5 August 1937.

A little over two months later, on 19 October, Montgomery's wife Betty died suddenly, the victim of an infected insect bite. He had married her while at Camberley, on 27 July 1927, and she had given birth to his son David just over a year later. Montgomery had been devoted to his wife, who had introduced him to a wide cultural circle and done much to bring him out of his social shell. Her death, therefore, plunged him into a deep loneliness and left with a nine-year-old son and two stepsons, both of whom were in the army, Montgomery once more hid behind a dedication to his profession that did much to alienate him from his peers.

With the approach of war in 1939, Montgomery found himself, once more, in Palestine, commanding the 8th Division at the rank of Major-General and charged with enforcing the British 'mandatory' authority over the region. Before long, however, he became ill and returned home in July where, upon his recovery, he took command of the 3rd Division on 28 August, just as war seemed imminent. His appointment had been secured under the influence of Brooke, who had been his fellow instructor at Camberley and was now a corps commander, and, on 30 September 1939, Montgomery landed with his new division in France.

As part of General Lord Gort's British Expeditionary Force (BEF), Montgomery spent the 'phoney-war' training his division to a very high level and it soon became one of the few crack formations within the British Army. During this period, Montgomery also evolved his trademark air of self-confidence and calm whatever the situation, as well as an idiosyncratic daily routine, which ended with an early bed-time. When the war began in earnest, with the German invasion of the Low Countries and France on 10 May 1940, the 3rd Division displayed the fruits of Montgomery's labour with a textbook advance to its pre-planned position at Louvain on the River Dyle in Belgium. Montgomery's division engaged in little actual fighting in its defence of Louvain before the BEF began its general withdrawal.

Nevertheless, during his retreat to the Dunkirk perimeter, Montgomery skilfully switched his division from one flank to the other at short notice and once within the Dunkirk beachhead, was given command of II Corps upon Brooke's evacuation to England. Before his own evacuation on 1 June, Montgomery successfully prevented the Germans from out-flanking the beachhead and co-ordinated the rearguard that protected the seaborne rescue of the BEF.

Following his experiences in France, Montgomery, now back in command of 3rd Division, resisted orders to deploy his men along the coastal defences and the 'stop-lines' behind them, believing that a

OVERLEAF: **Montgomery as commander of XII Corps during army exercises, 1942.**

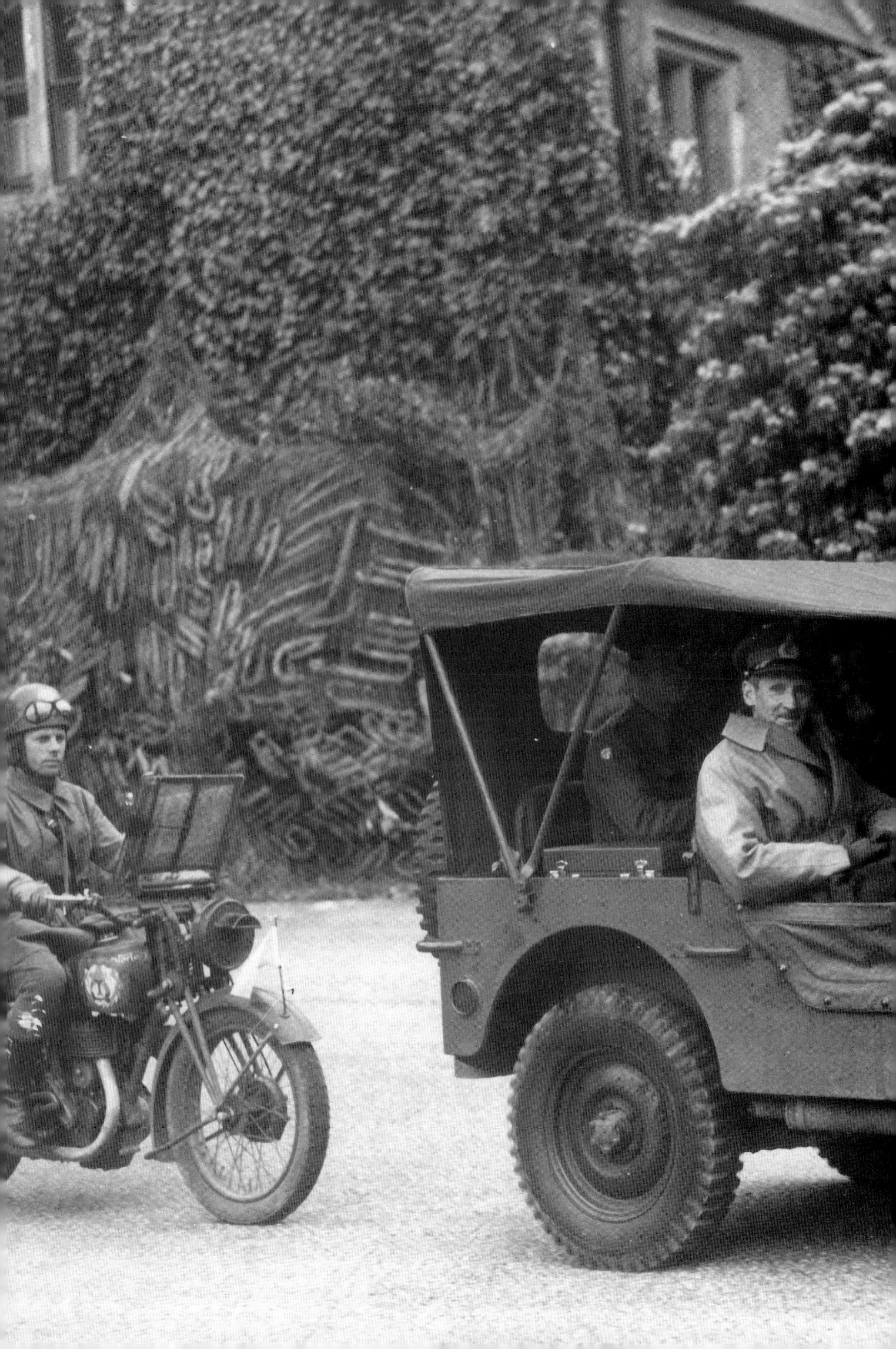

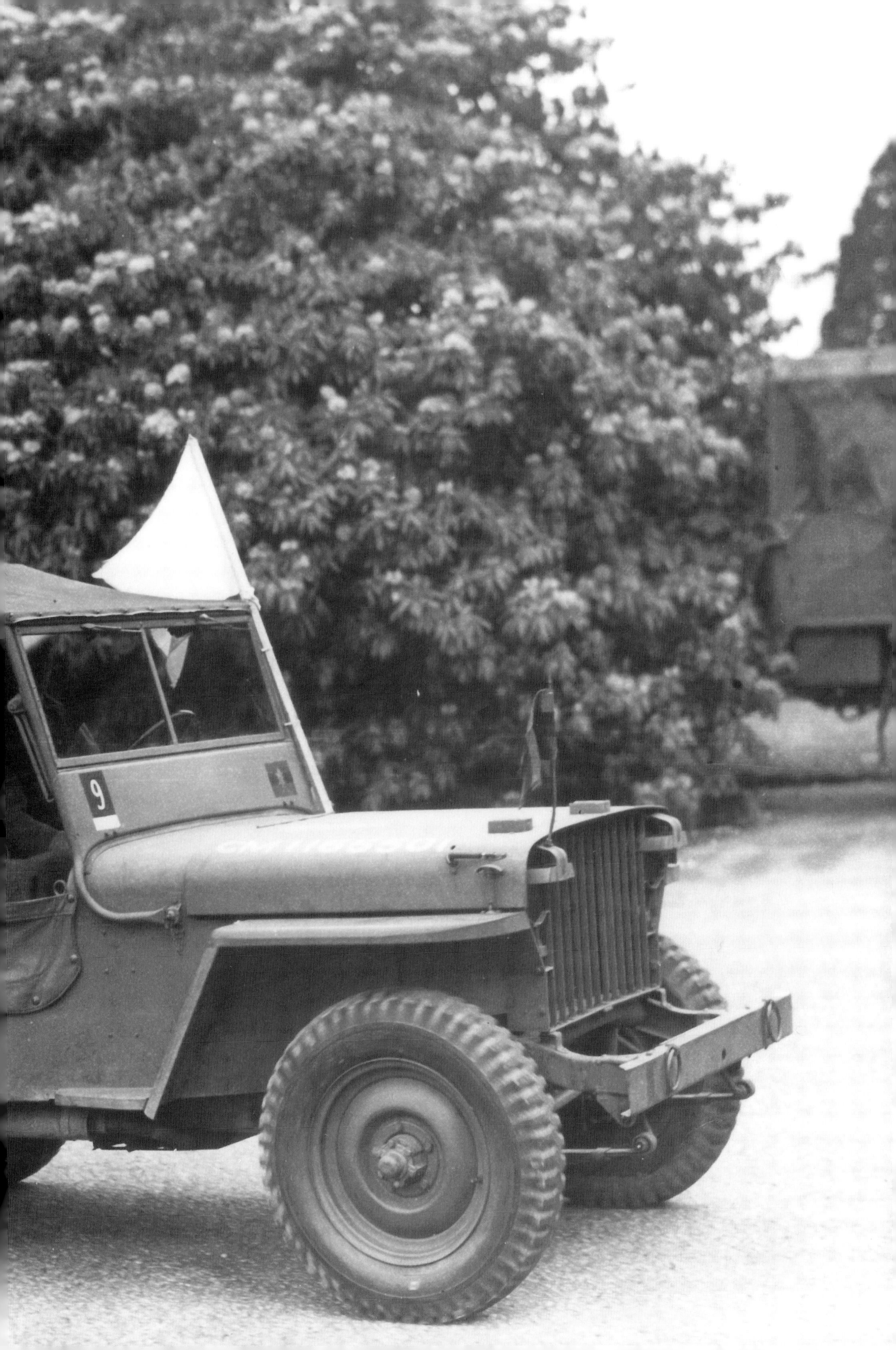
9

purely defensive posture, should invasion come, would merely invite disaster. He hankered after a mobile counter-attack role instead and upset his superiors when he courted Prime Minister Churchill's support. He persisted on this issue upon his promotion to Lieutenant-General and command of V Corps on 22 July 1940, which caused many bitter clashes with his superior, Claude Auchinleck, Commander-in-Chief of Southern Command. Nevertheless, in April 1941, when he was transferred to command XII Corps, Montgomery was one of the first to acknowledge that the threat of invasion had finally passed. He began to instil a new offensive spirit in his men, the key to which, he believed, was maintaining their morale. Moreover, Montgomery once again displayed his penchant for training, his belief in the importance of which made him stand out from so many of his contemporaries. However, his unorthodox methods, such as forcing elderly colonels to undertake forced marches, did not endear him to his peers. Indeed, Montgomery's contempt for their criticism and his own flair for self-advertisement, meant that despite his obvious qualities, he was not a natural selection for army command.

However, Montgomery still had friends in high places, most notably Brooke who at the end of 1941, had become Chief of the Imperial General Staff. Brooke's confidence in Montgomery was instrumental in ensuring that the latter was chosen as a replacement for Lieutenant-General William 'Strafer' Gott, who had been killed while en route to take command of Eighth Army in Egypt. Hence, on 13 August 1942, Montgomery took over the army's most prestigious command at the time of its greatest peril. More by luck than judgment, Montgomery now had the opportunity to make his mark and enhance his reputation still further.

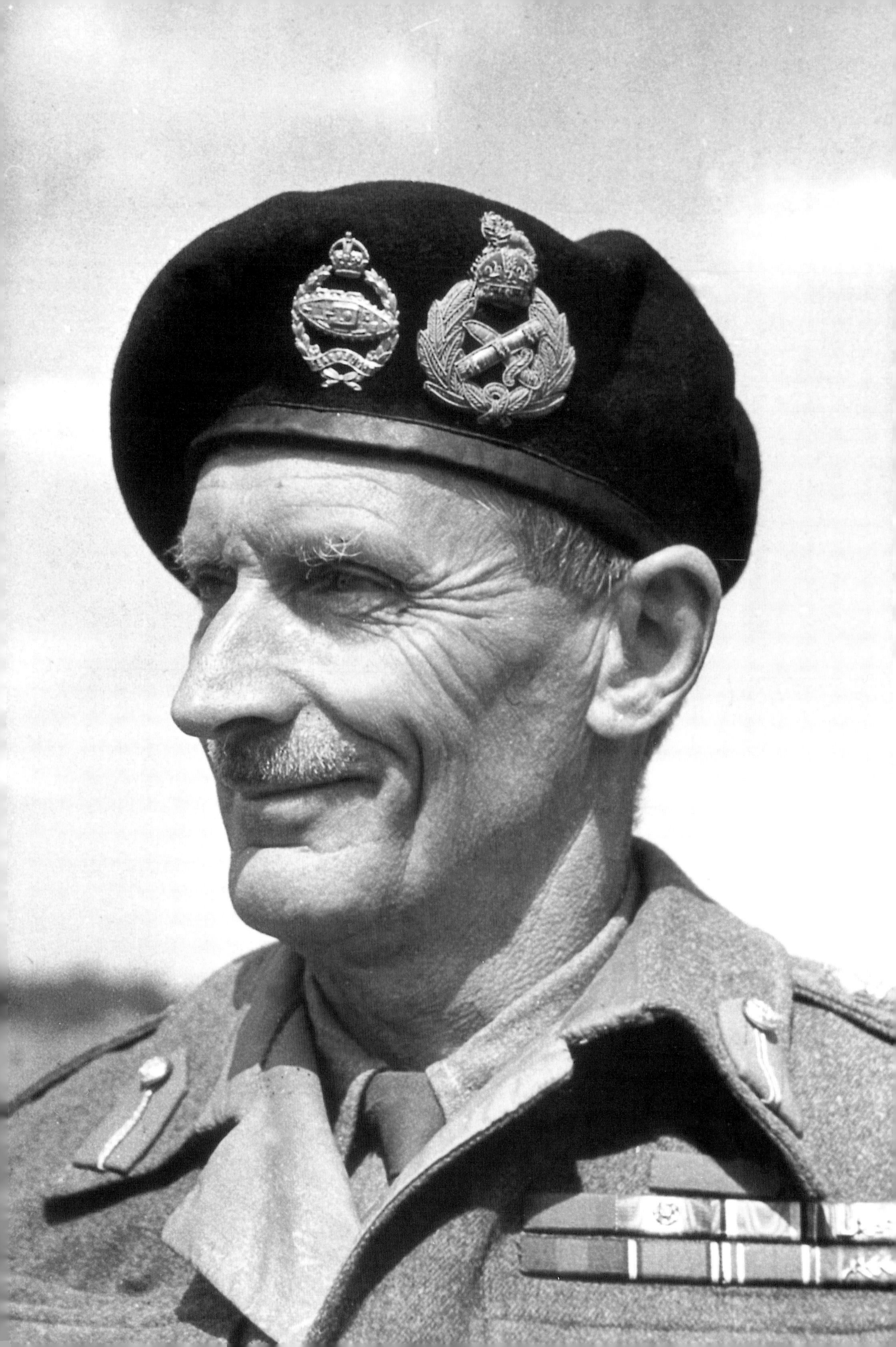

CHAPTER 2

VICTORY AT EL ALAMEIN

At the time of Montgomery's arrival, Eighth Army was in a parlous state. Recently defeated by Field-Marshal Erwin Rommel at the battle of Gazala, which had resulted in the humiliating loss of Tobruk, it had been forced to retreat to the El Alamein line, a mere sixty miles from Alexandria. Here, Montgomery's immediate predecessor, his old sparring partner Auchinleck, had halted Rommel at the first battle of El Alamein. Auchinleck's victory was nevertheless a limited one. Rommel had been merely halted, not pushed back, and this was not enough to satisfy Churchill, who removed Auchinleck from command.

LEFT: **Field Marshal Montgomery of Alamein, wearing the cap he made famous, although it had been the official head-dress of the Royal Tank Regiment since 1925.**

Flying out from Britain to assume his new command two days early, Montgomery declared that he had little time for the 'bad old ways' of his predecessors. Aided by an old acquaintance, Freddie de Guingand, who became his Chief of Staff, Montgomery soon imposed his will on Eighth Army headquarters. Co-locating the headquarters of the Desert Air Force with his own and replacing key individuals with his own hand-picked men, he informed his subordinates that he would countenance no retreat from El Alamein. This assertion was to be tested one more time by Rommel, before his material strength was completely dwarfed by that of Eighth Army. During the course of August, British tank strength had increased to almost 700, while three out of every four convoys bound for Rommel were successfully intercepted. Rommel consequently received meagre reinforcements of fuel, ammunition and infantry, but no armour. Nevertheless, he still had over 400 tanks at his disposal and ten divisions to Montgomery's seven. He therefore resolved to launch one last effort to pierce Eighth Army's line. On the night of 30 August, Rommel began a local offensive with the intention of turning the British southern flank with his armoured formations. He then aimed to advance some 30 miles before turning north to attack Eighth Army's supply area on the coast.

Montgomery was, however, well prepared. Warned of the timing of Rommel's attack by British intelligence, Montgomery made slight modifications to the defensive plan he had inherited from Auchinleck, one which correctly anticipated Rommel's battle-plan and which relied heavily on artillery and dug-in tanks. Rommel was allowed to make his flanking attack, but his armoured units, held up by the unexpected depth of the British minefields, were gradually funnelled towards British positions on the Alam Halfa ridge. By first light on the 31st, Rommel's spearhead had advanced only eight miles, was under heavy air attack and hampered by fuel shortages.

His attack soon foundered on the Alam Halfa ridge. Having lost fifty tanks and realizing the vulnerability of his position, Rommel ordered a gradual withdrawal on 2 September. Four days later, Rommel's forces were back on their start line and shielded by minefields.

The battle of Alam Halfa proved to be Rommel's last hurrah in the desert war. The plan worked out by Auchinleck and refined by Montgomery had worked beautifully, yet Churchill criticized Montgomery for not being aggressive enough during the battle. The latter had attempted a counter-attack, but its ineffectiveness had convinced Montgomery that Eighth Army required extensive training before launching the set-piece battle he believed was necessary to penetrate Rommel's defences. Codenamed Lightfoot, the offensive would not be launched until the next full-moon period as Montgomery felt that daylight attacks by the infantry in the desert were close to suicide.

ABOVE: **Captured German troops head into captivity.**

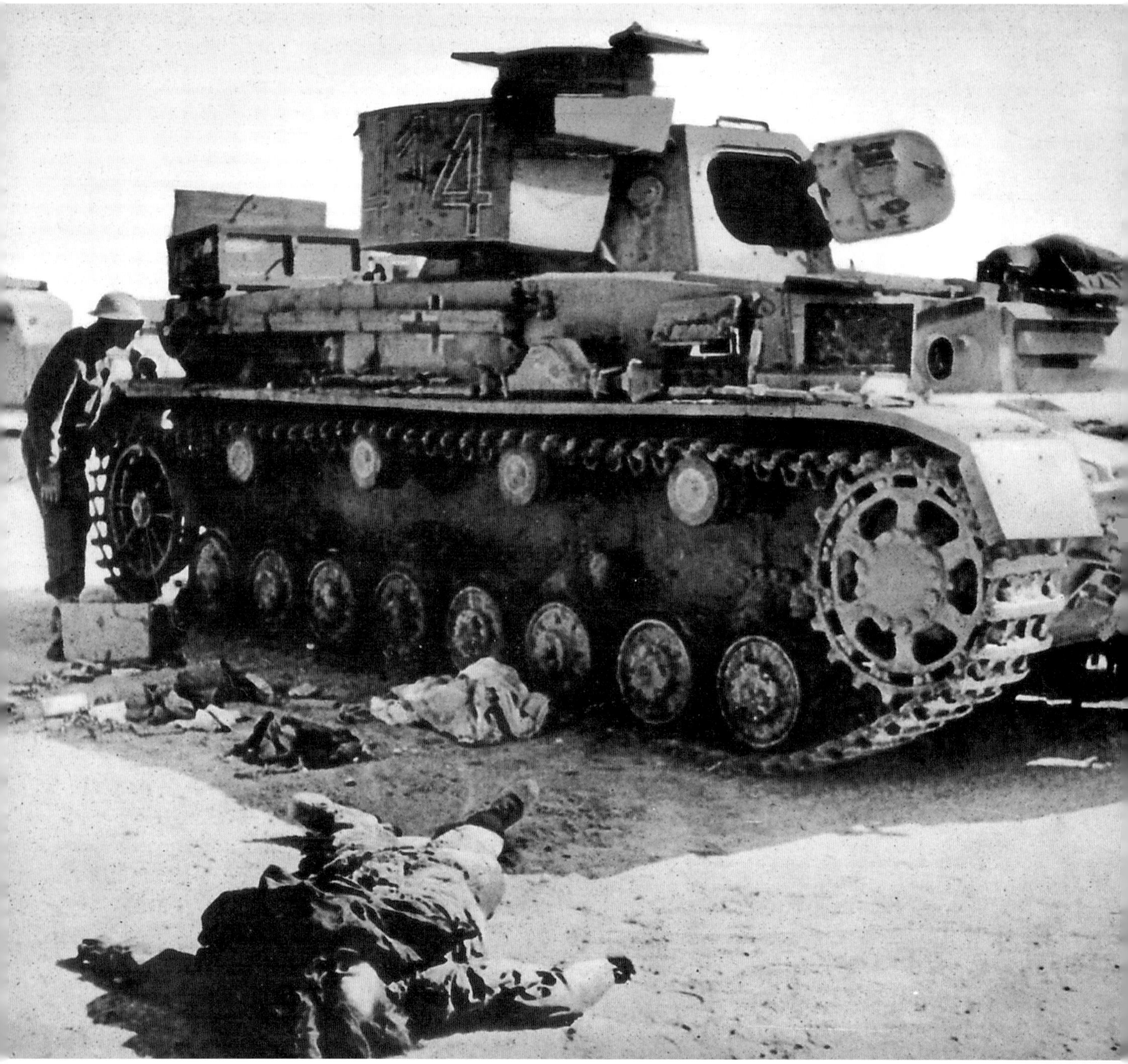

Upon his arrival, Montgomery had been highly critical of Eighth Army's poor morale and training, which took the form of disparaging remarks concerning Auchinleck's period of command. Unfortunate though these were, there was little doubt that the morale of the troops had suffered from constantly moving back and forth across the desert, while their poor level of training had all too often been exposed by Rommel. With his penchant for self-publicity, Montgomery soon proved capable of inspiring his army, largely through the deliberate cultivation of what became known as the 'Monty cult', which was given expression by his own informal dress and his distinctive beret adorned by two regimental badges. This was to counter the almost mythological status that Rommel had acquired within Eighth Army and by making countless visits to the units under his command, Montgomery began to instil a new spirit within

LEFT: **The aftermath of a desert tank battle. A knocked out German PzIV tank sits beside the body of one of its crew.**

Eighth Army's ranks. More information was imparted throughout the chain of command, especially concerning the part each unit would play in the forthcoming offensive. A thorough training programme was initiated to train the men in all aspects of battlecraft, particularly the difficult job of clearing gaps through minefields. Meanwhile, patrols and small probing operations were conducted for the purpose of gaining intelligence on enemy positions. This was supplemented by the use of ground and air reconnaissance to map out Rommel's defensive positions. Finally, Montgomery sanctioned a number of local attacks, with mixed results, in order to test the strength of these positions and secure better jumping-off points for the main offensive. While his men were being put through their paces, Montgomery decided that his great offensive, which would 'hit Rommel for six right out of Africa', would commence on the night of 23 October 1942.

The El Alamein position was bordered by the sea to the north and the impassable Qattara Depression to the south, and the 37-mile-long front was therefore not susceptible to the favoured desert tactic of turning the enemy's southern flank with mobile forces. Montgomery's final plan for the battle, issued on 6 October, therefore envisaged a direct frontal assault against the northern part of Rommel's line. Moreover, Montgomery felt that an attritional battle was more suited to British military strengths, while also restricting the mobility of Rommel's armoured divisions. Rather than chase Rommel's army back towards Tripoli, Montgomery hoped instead to engage it in a set-piece battle and destroy its offensive capability once and for all.

Since the battle of Alam Halfa, the Axis forces had dug themselves in to a considerable degree and these defences had to be destroyed

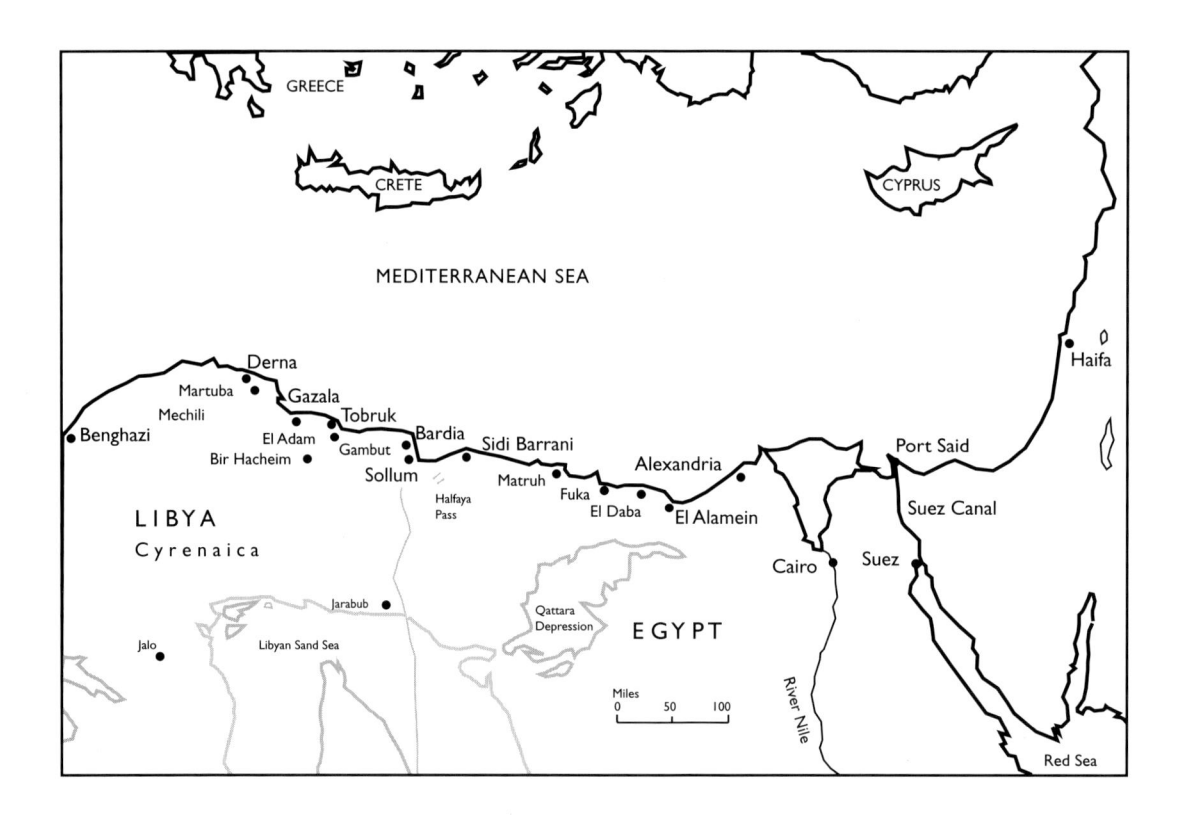

ABOVE: **The Western Desert theatre.**

before any breakthrough could be attempted. Accordingly, Montgomery planned to open the battle with a massive artillery bombardment, followed by an infantry assault against the enemy line to the north. This was to be conducted by XXX Corps, commanded by Lieutenant-General Sir Oliver Leese. Meanwhile, sappers would open up two corridors in the Axis minefields through which would drive the armoured divisions of X Corps, under the command of Lieutenant-General Herbert Lumsden. Once XXX Corps had formed a breach, it would continue, as Montgomery put it, to 'crumble' the enemy infantry formations holding the minefields, by wearing them down with force of firepower until they gave way. At this point, X Corps would punch through the gaps created in the minefields and engage and destroy Rommel's armour by taking up defensive positions with XXX Corps' infantry and awaiting the inevitable counter-attack from the Axis armour. The resulting battle of attrition, which Montgomery labelled the 'dogfight', would eventually blast a hole through the northern centre of Rommel's line, through which Eighth Army would break out into open desert.

RIGHT: **Montgomery visits British armoured troops in the forward area to present awards for gallantry, January 1943.**

VICTORY AT EL ALAMEIN

During the crucial first phase of the battle, elements of XIII Corps, commanded by Lieutenant-General Brian Horrocks, would launch diversionary attacks in the southern sector of the line. Designed to hold part of Rommel's armour away from the main fighting to the north, XIII Corps' attack was part of an elaborate deception plan which aimed to convince Rommel that the main British thrust would, once again, involve an armoured sweep around his southern flank. The deception also involved populating the southern sector with dummy tanks and vehicles, the construction of a fake fuel pipeline and the use of false radio traffic. Montgomery's plan was simple in its conception and he estimated that it would take 12 days to execute.

In making these plans, Montgomery had the luxury of knowing that Eighth Army had built up a clear numerical and material advantage over the forces at Rommel's disposal. Included in this superiority were significant amounts of American equipment, including 300 of the new M-4 Sherman tanks. These arrived in September and added to what was, on paper, a formidable advantage for Montgomery at every level. By mid-October, Eighth Army deployed 11 divisions, including four armoured, totalling 230,000 men, which opposed just 80,000 men under Rommel, of which 53,000 were Italians. These were backed up by 530 serviceable aircraft against just 350, only 150 of which were German models, and 2,311 guns of all types against 1,368, again the majority of which were of Italian manufacture. The biggest discrepancy was in tanks: 1,029 tanks, plus more in reserve, opposed only 489, including a mere 211 German types. Montgomery's attritional battle-plan indeed relied and depended upon this overwhelming surfeit of resources and in the circumstances, to attempt any risky manoeuvres would have squandered these advantages.

The preliminary phase of Montgomery's offensive got under way on 19 October, when the Desert Air Force attacked enemy airfields. These raids helped secure air superiority for the British throughout the duration of the battle. The main battle commenced, as planned, at 9.40pm on 23 October, when almost all of Montgomery's artillery opened up along the front. Although the enemy had long expected an attack, the timing had been successfully concealed from them and the largest artillery bombardment since the First World War took them completely by surprise. Consequently, their response was initially slow and confused and XXX Corps made good early progress. However, Rommel's infantry soon recovered their composure and as their resistance stiffened, heavy and confused fighting descended on the front. By dawn on 24 October, while some divisions had reached their objectives, the remainder had been prevented from doing so and had suffered considerable casualties.

Meanwhile, the sappers and pioneers charged with creating corridors through the enemy minefields were encountering problems of their own. Their new mine-detecting equipment soon proved ineffective and they were forced to return to the traditional method of prodding for mines with a bayonet. Consequently, by the morning of the 24th, fewer gaps had been created than was hoped for and the progress of the armoured divisions was further delayed by dust, congestion and misdirection, which exposed them to concerted enemy anti-tank and artillery fire.

Despite these problems, Montgomery ordered the 'break-in' phase to continue, although during the course of the first day the fighting had degenerated into a straightforward slugging match. Nevertheless, that evening, Montgomery informed his corps commanders of his determination to stick to the original plan. Meanwhile, as planned, diversionary attacks had been mounted in the southern sector by elements of XIII Corps. These too ran into difficulties and although their efforts had succeeded in keeping two of Rommel's divisions away from the main battle, no enemy forces had been drawn away from the crucial sector. Montgomery had by this time been forced to concede that his initial breakout plan had failed. The minefields had been too deep to clear in one night and this had left his tanks penned in and exposed to the full force of Rommel's defences.

Nevertheless, Eighth Army's efforts had left the Axis forces in a certain amount of disarray and on the evening of the 25th, Montgomery switched the emphasis of his attack to the northern part of the line in an attempt to cut the coast road behind enemy lines. By shifting his thrust lines, Montgomery hoped to exploit one of Rommel's major weaknesses, his shortage of fuel. Meanwhile, during the course of 26 October, Montgomery continued the process of 'crumbling' the enemy line in the centre of the northern sector. Bringing up reinforcements from XIII Corps to the south, Montgomery ruthlessly applied his superiority in numbers and fire-power to batter the enemy line. During the next few days, the Axis forces were subjected to a succession of heavy artillery bombardments, air attacks and limited infantry thrusts. Montgomery's 'dogfight' stage of the battle was met by a succession of concerted Axis armoured counter-attacks ordered by Rommel, who, after his return from sick-leave, had by now grasped the seriousness of his situation.

OVERLEAF: **Montgomery visits Benghazi after its capture in December 1942, where he enjoys a meal of bully beef and tinned potatoes.**

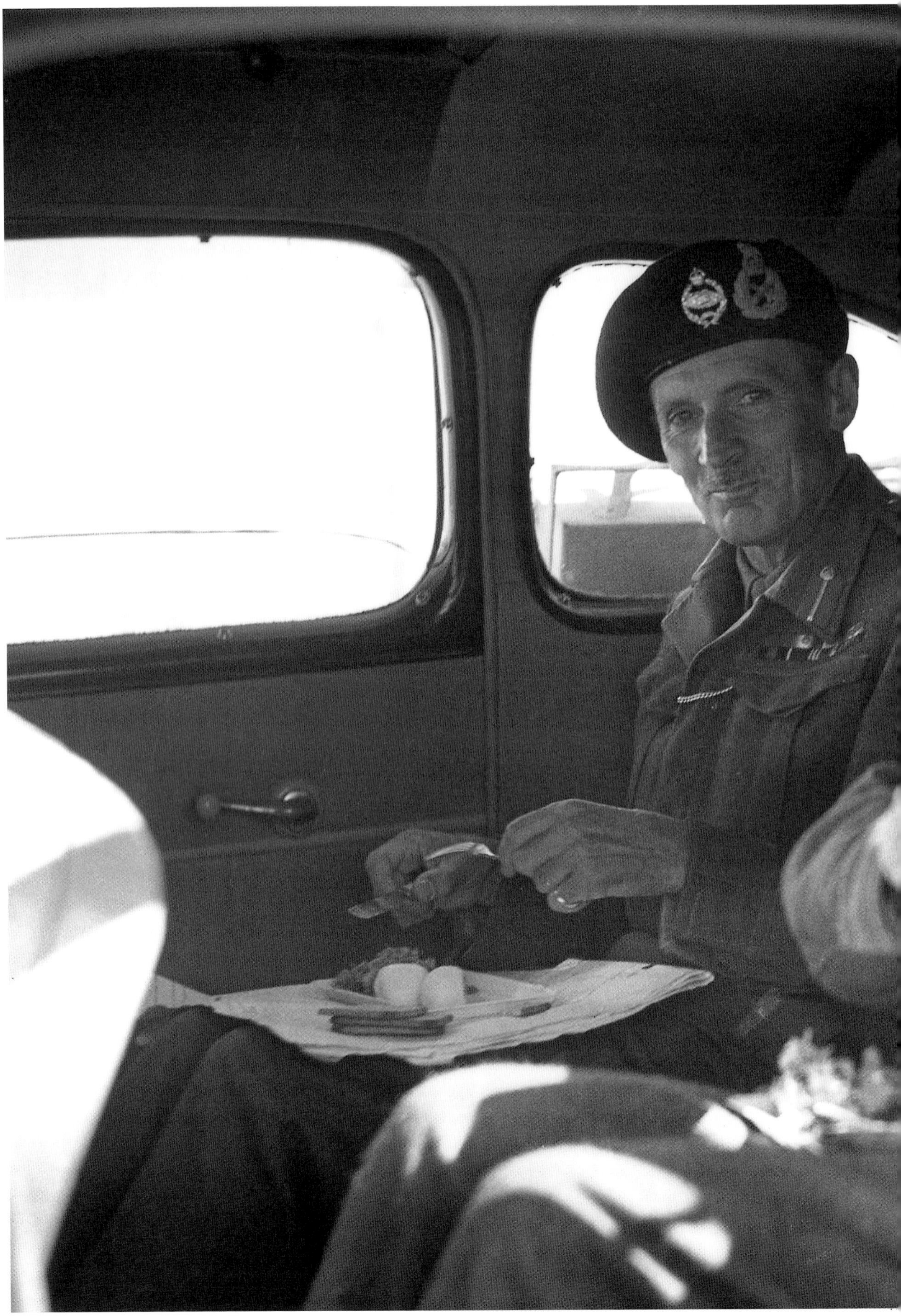

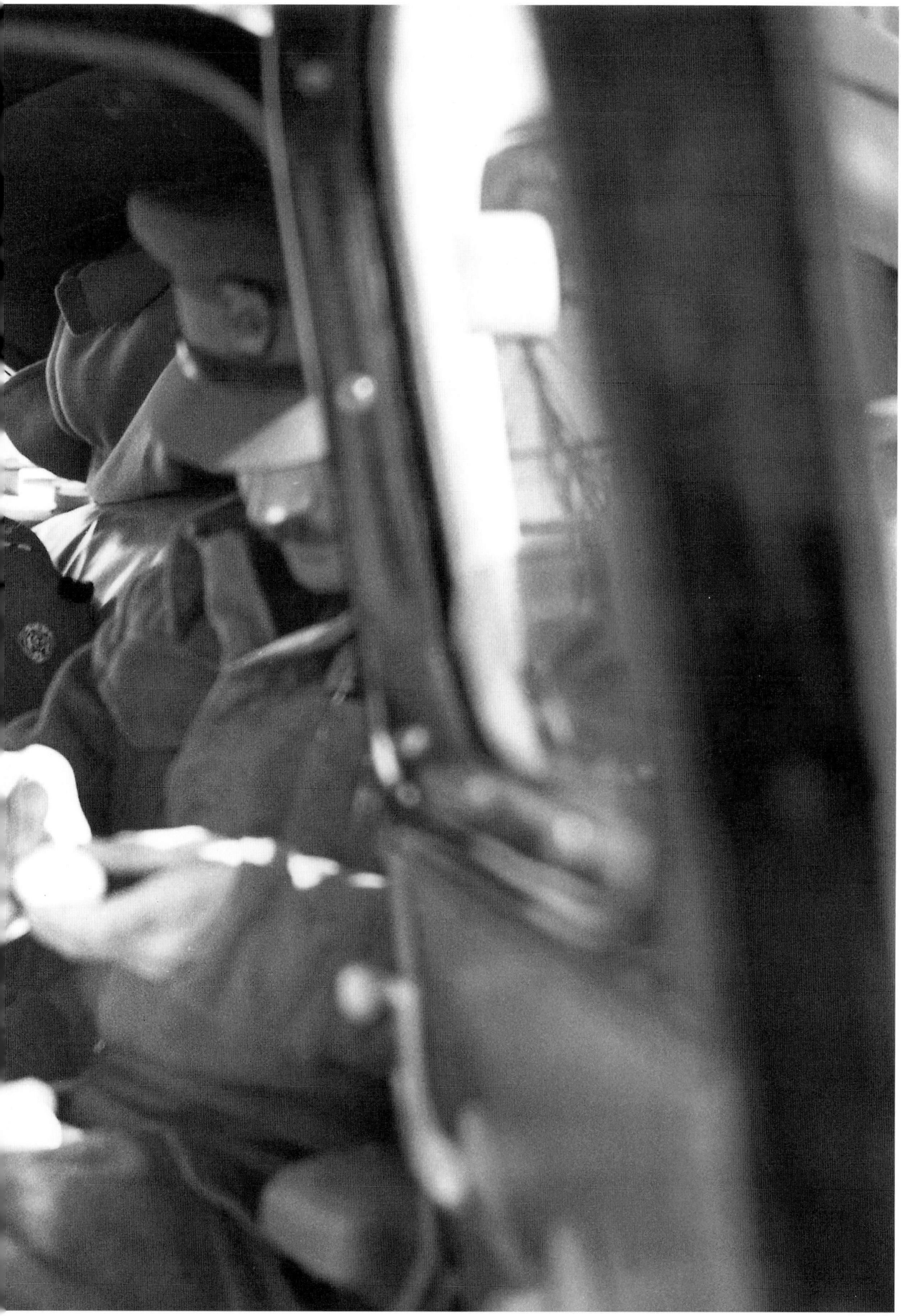

This passage of the battle proved successful in wearing down Rommel's forces, but at no little cost to Eighth Army. During the first week of the offensive, Montgomery had lost four times as many tanks as Rommel but, crucially, still had 800 available; roughly eight times more than Rommel had remaining at his disposal. Nevertheless, Eighth Army had still made little headway and the mounting casualties and incessant fighting obliged Montgomery to call a temporary halt to his offensive. He now regrouped his rather disorganized forces, withdrawing elements of XXX Corps to form a reserve for a new plan, codenamed Operation Supercharge.

Montgomery intended Supercharge to be the final breakout and it was essentially a modified version of his original plan. Once again, a formidable artillery barrage would herald an initial infantry attack to breach Rommel's line, through which Montgomery's armour would then pass and destroy the remainder of Rommel's forces. Supercharge was launched at 1.05am on 2 November. A total of 800 guns opened up along a frontage of only 4,000 yards. The infantry attack was entrusted to Major-General Bernard Freyberg, commander of the 2nd New Zealand Division, which was reinforced by two British infantry brigades. Backed up by huge artillery support, Freyberg rapidly penetrated deep inside the weakened Axis line. The following armoured attack was assigned to the 9th Armoured Brigade whose commander, Brigadier John Currie, was told by Montgomery to accept, if necessary, one hundred per cent casualties to achieve his objective. This was to assault Rommel's artillery and anti-tank screen just before dawn and force a breach, which would then be exploited by the 1st Armoured Division. Currie's attack was, however, delayed by thirty minutes, so that when he reached Rommel's gun line his tanks became silhouetted by first light, making them perfect targets for the enemy gunners. Within minutes, the brigade was decimated and had lost 70 out of its 94 tanks by the end of the day. It had, however, managed to destroy 35 tanks and guns during its sacrificial attack, hardware that Rommel could ill-afford to lose.

Moreover, 9th Armoured Brigade's attack had created much confusion amongst the Axis ranks, which 1st Armoured Division was meant to capitalize on. In the event, severe vehicle congestion, described by one infantryman as 'like Piccadilly Circus at rush hour', delayed the division's approach march and caused problems in its deployment. Eventually, the British armour was able to deploy in the gap created in Rommel's gun screen, taking up defensive positions under cover of the British artillery. They were now ready to meet Rommel's expected counter-attack. Rommel duly obliged by launching a series of desperate counter-attacks throughout the day. By nightfall, the ferocity of Rommel's attacks had nevertheless failed to dislodge the British armour which, in tandem with the Desert Air

Force, had in turn inflicted severe carnage on the Axis formations. In total, 70 German and 47 Italian tanks lay wrecked on the battlefield and Rommel was forced to concede defeat. Eighth Army's breakout had indeed been held, but at such cost that Rommel had only 35 serviceable tanks remaining, and these were desperately short of fuel. Accordingly, he ordered a withdrawal along the coast to Fuka, some 60 miles west of Alamein.

The following day, fighting continued as Eighth Army, aware that a withdrawal was under way, tried unsuccessfully to pierce Rommel's powerful rearguard. At this point, Rommel received a message direct from Hitler, ordering him not to withdraw. An unbelieving Rommel nevertheless obeyed and countermanded as many retreat orders as

OVERLEAF: **Montgomery is presented with an autographed portrait of the Chinese leader, Generalissimo Chiang Kai Shek, by Chinese generals visiting the Middle East.**

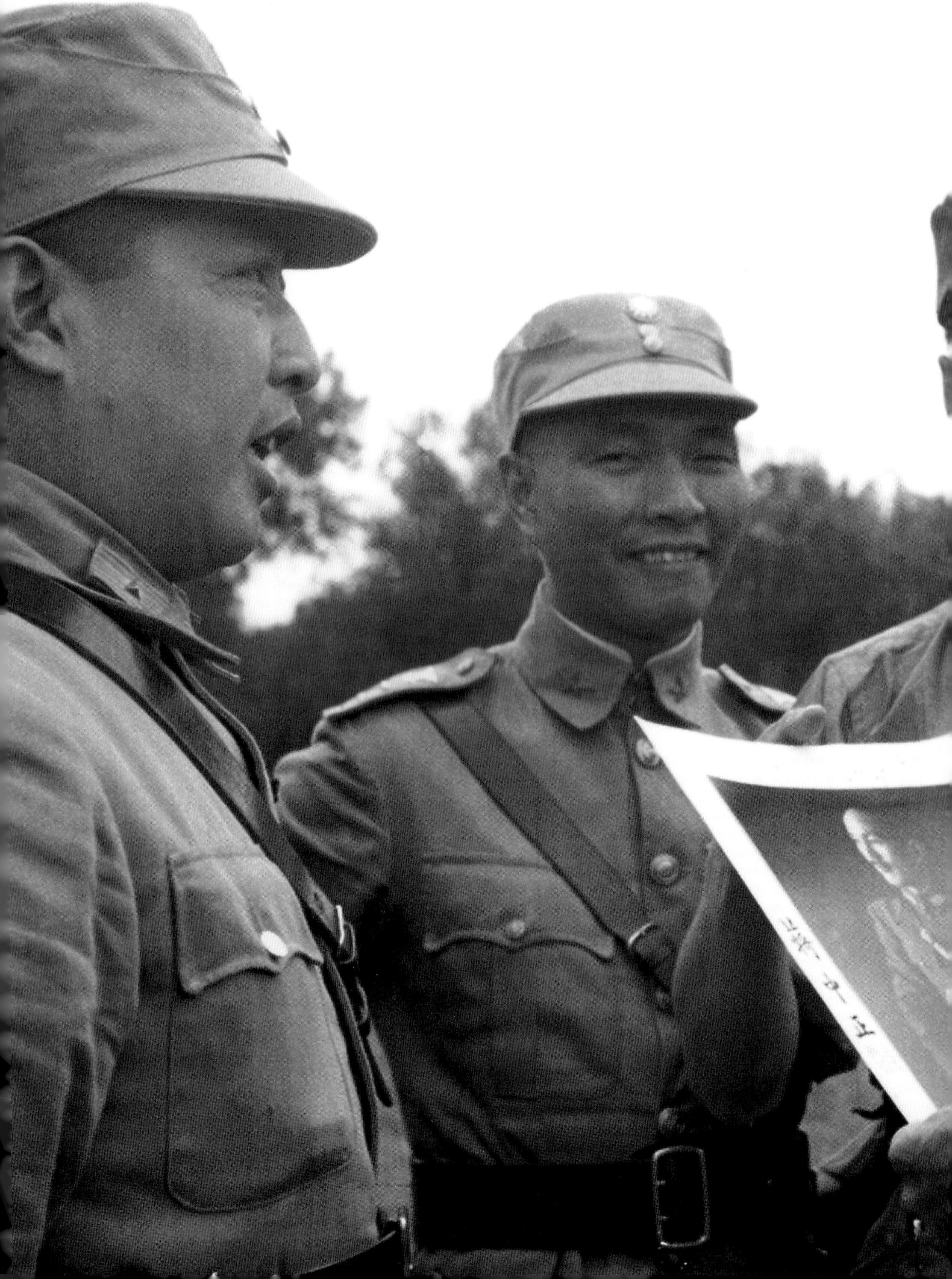

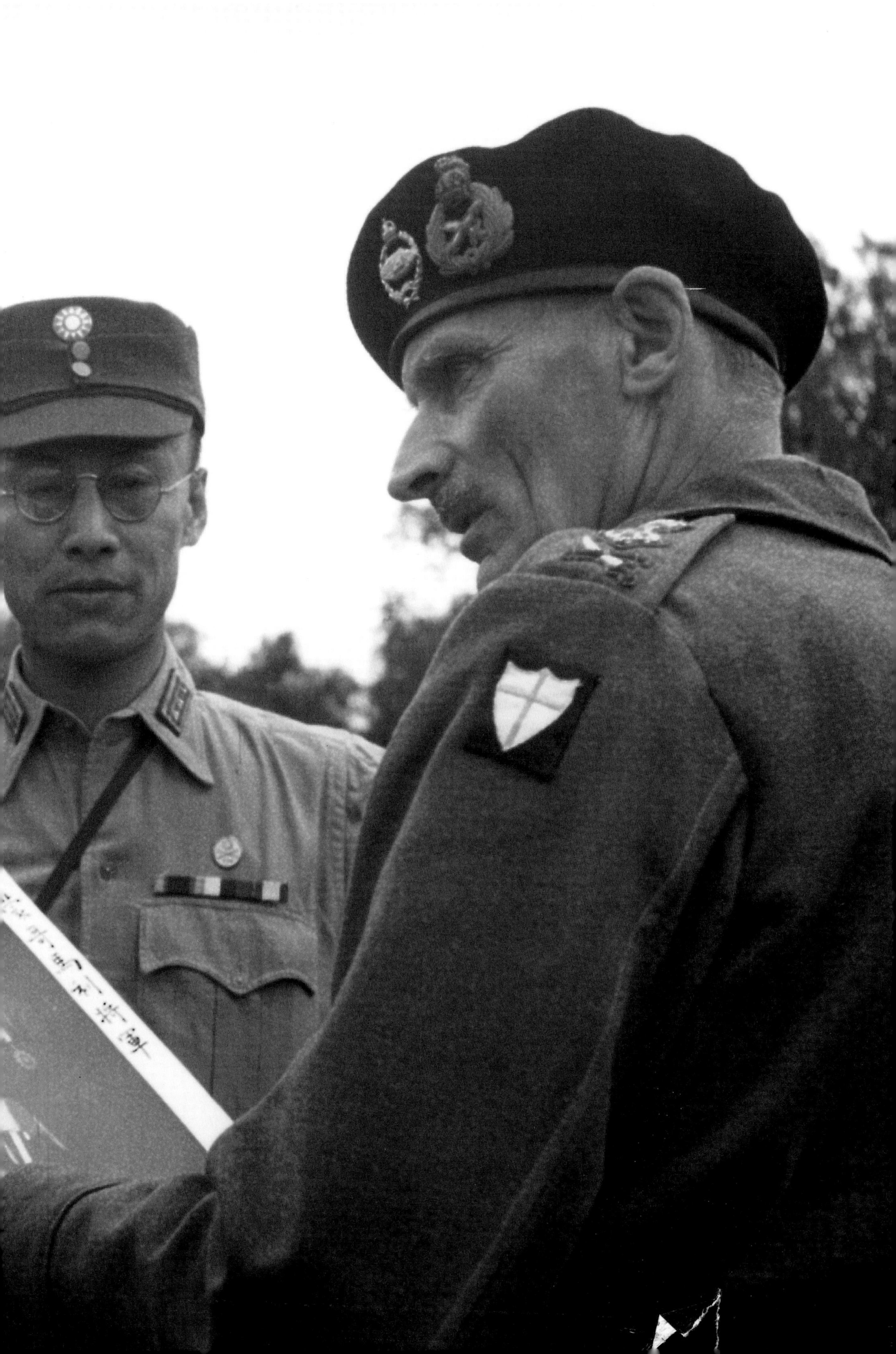

possible, and committed his remaining strength to holding the northernmost section of the line. Regularly and quickly informed of the fluctuations in Rommel's intentions by British intelligence, Montgomery switched his pressure to the now weakened centre of the northern sector of the Axis line. Finally, on 4 November, his infantry created further ruptures in the Axis defences, and his armoured divisions poured through the breach in pursuit. The delay caused by Hitler's intervention had prevented Rommel from making a stand at Fuka and, although he managed to extricate his most valuable troops, he had only twelve tanks left fit for action and large numbers of Axis prisoners were bagged by the advancing Eighth Army.

RIGHT: **Montgomery's adversary, Field-Marshal Erwin Rommel.**

VICTORY AT EL ALAMEIN

MONTY

Despite Rommel's escape, Montgomery had nevertheless secured a major victory. The battle had by no means followed Montgomery's master-plan, but had been concluded in the 12 days he had forecast it would take. The clear numerical and material superiority enjoyed by Eighth Army had undoubtedly been a major factor, but so too was Montgomery's thorough preparation of his forces and his flexibility during the battle. Montgomery had warned that his offensive would 'involve hard and prolonged fighting' and this prediction was certainly borne out. Eighth Army casualties had reached 13,560, only five per cent of its total strength, but a quarter of

LEFT: **Montgomery's command tank, now on permanent display at the Imperial War Museum, London.**

OVERLEAF: **Montgomery in Cairo visiting his brother-in-law, Mr A Holding OBE, an official in the Egyptian Ministry of Finance. Mr and Mrs Holding followed Montgomery's career with great interest and were very proud of him.**

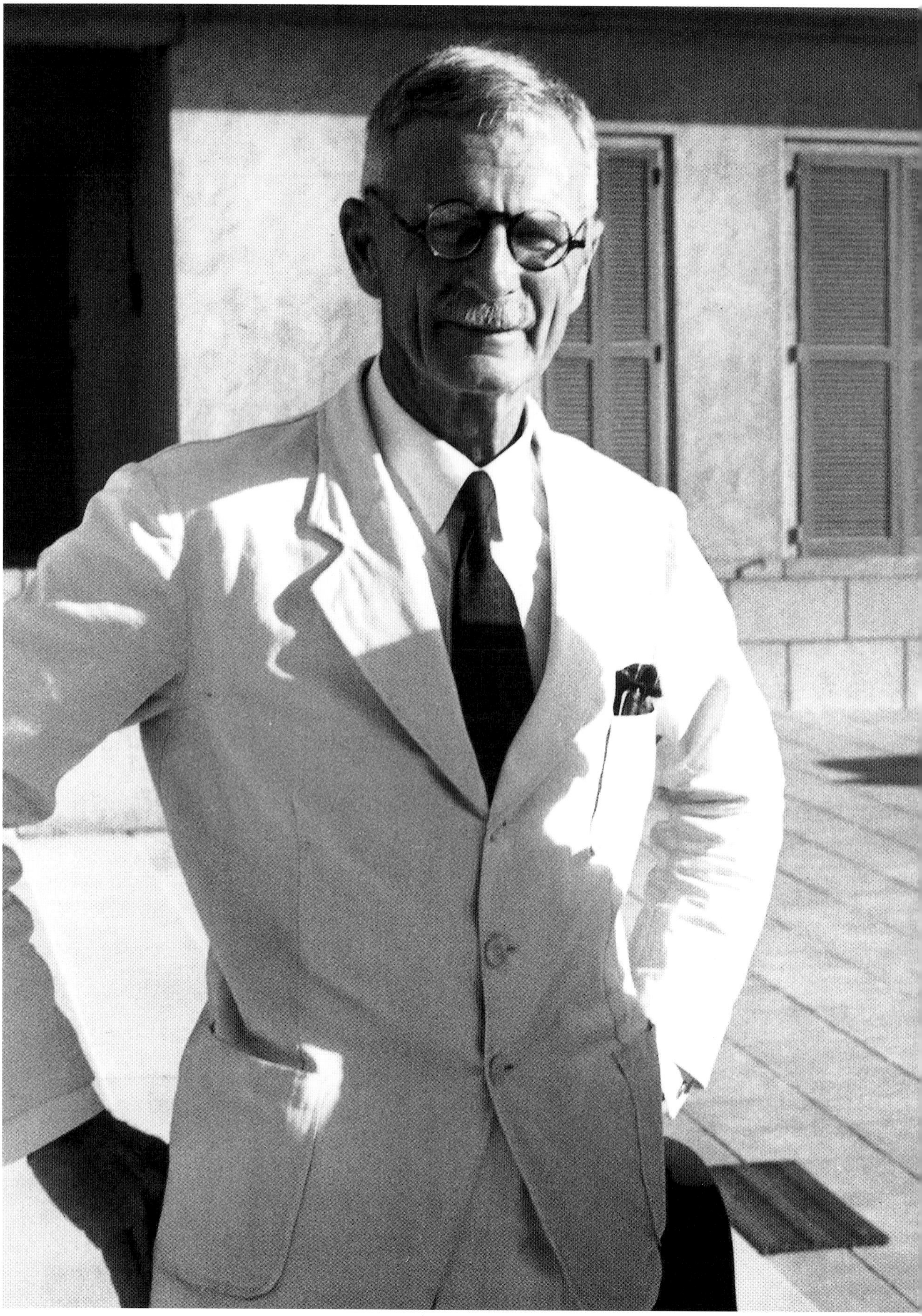

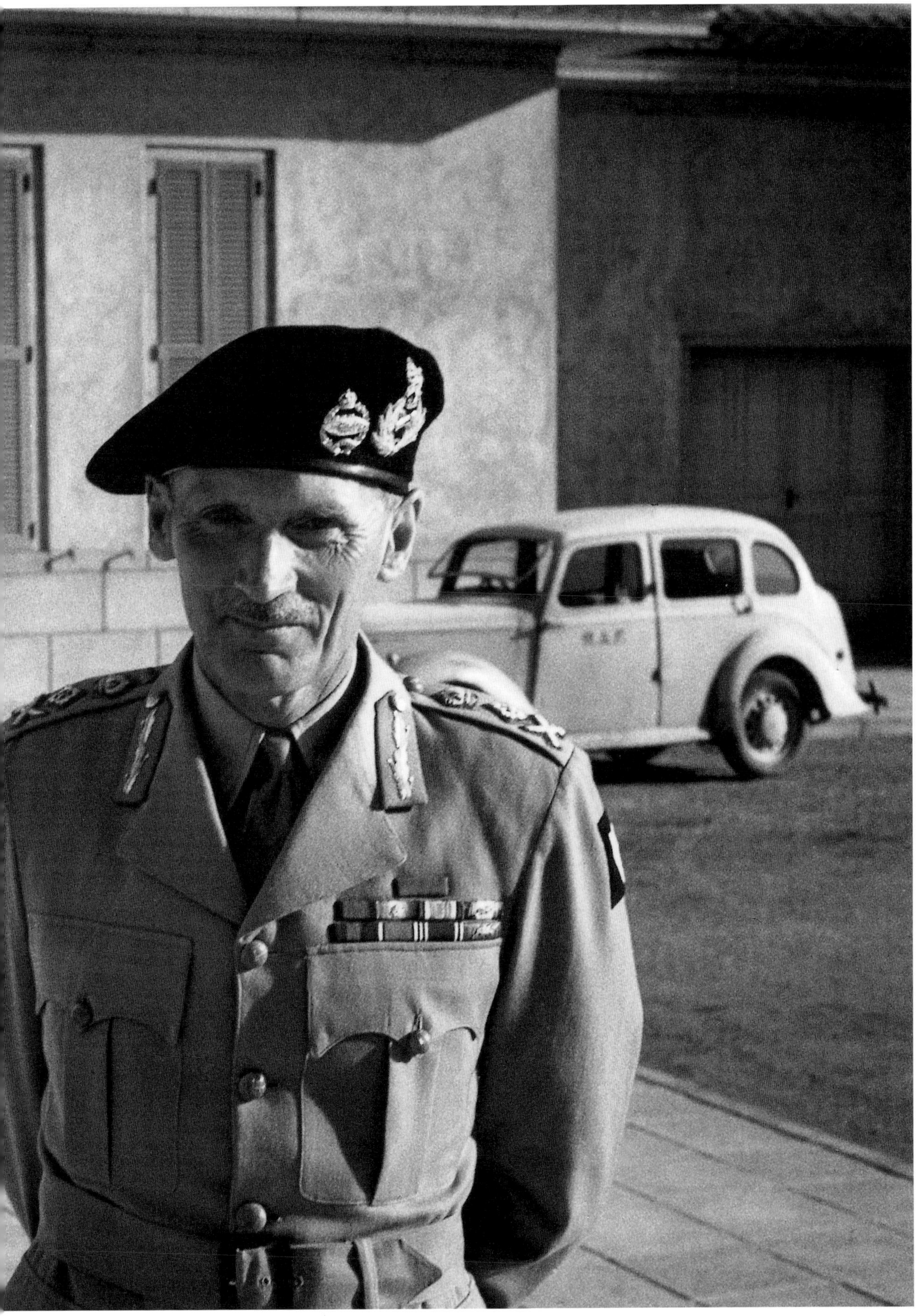

its infantry. Montgomery had almost exactly predicted this figure, which was nevertheless the highest toll suffered by a British army in the war to date. In addition, 500 tanks had been put out of action (although 300 of these were later recovered) and aircraft losses amounted to 928. Rommel's Panzer Army Afrika had, nonetheless, been smashed and over 35,000 prisoners captured. What was a comprehensive victory by any military standards was transformed into a decisive one just a few days later when, on 8 November, an Anglo-American army landed in Morocco and Algeria. Codenamed Operation Torch, this effectively condemned Rommel to a war on two fronts and he was forced to fall back to Tunisia, where he was finally to receive reinforcements.

Rommel was able to keep one step ahead of Eighth Army as he retreated across Libya, albeit under constant air attack from the

Desert Air Force. Kept at bay by a number of rearguard actions and the use of booby traps, Montgomery's advance across Libya was nevertheless a triumph of logistics. Tobruk was re-captured on 13 November, while Benghazi fell a week later. Each time Rommel made a stand, such as at El Agheila between 23 November and 13 December 1942 and Wadi Zem Zem from 26 December to 16 January 1943, concerted British pressure and lack of Axis resources forced Rommel to retreat still further. Finally, on 23 January 1943, Tripoli – for so long the ultimate goal of Eighth Army – was captured. While Montgomery paused to open the port up for resupply, Rommel, after a gruelling 2,000-mile retreat, crossed the Tunisian border three days later and rallied his army behind the Mareth Line. Libya was now completely in British hands and it only remained for Montgomery, in tandem with the forces landed by Torch, to expel Rommel from the shores of North Africa.

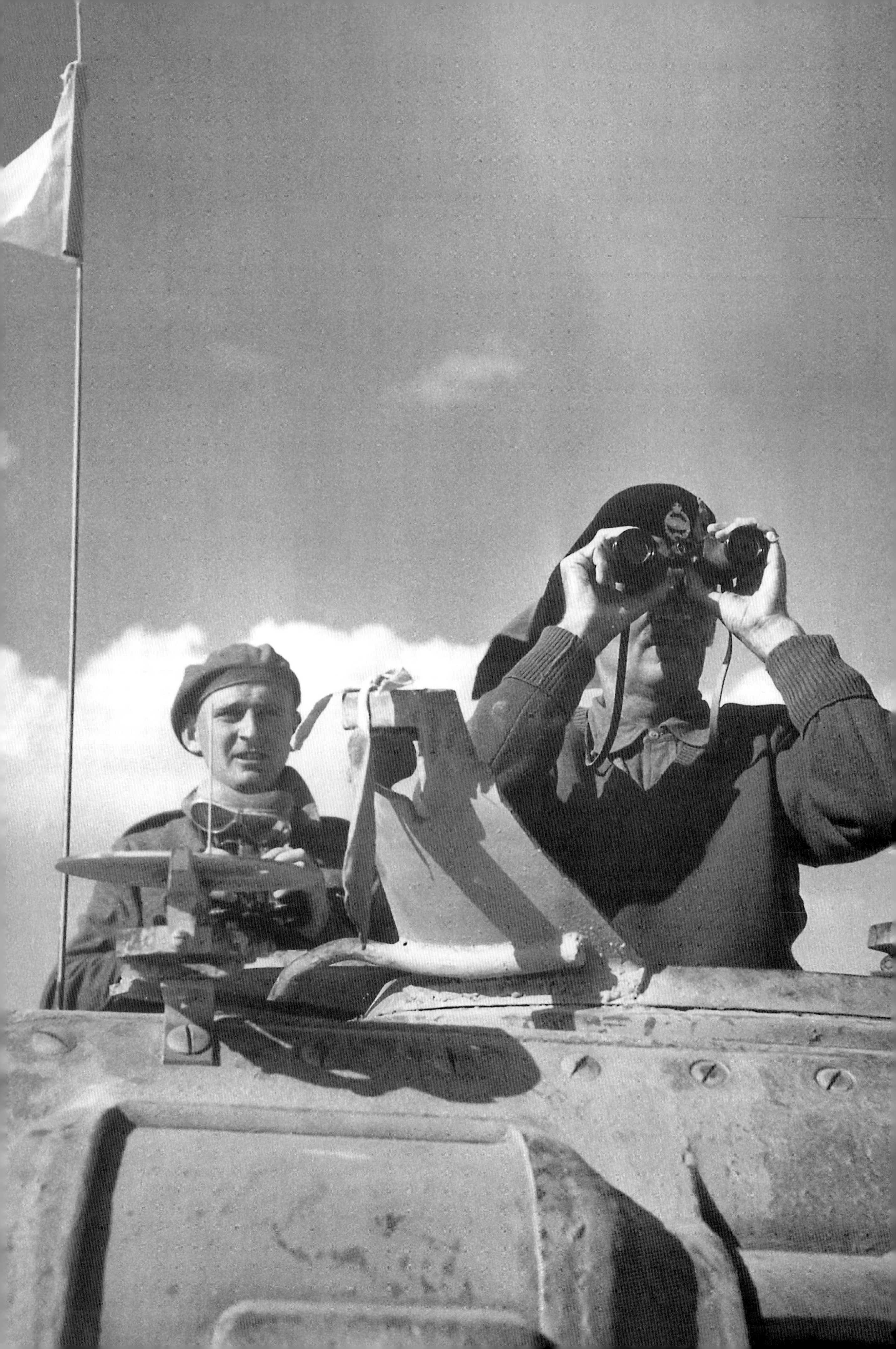

CHAPTER 3

FROM TUNISIA TO ITALY

O<small>NE WEEK AFTER HIS</small> victory at El Alamein had been completed, on 11 November 1942, Montgomery was promoted to full General and received a knighthood for 'distinguished service in the field'. Montgomery had finally delivered the victory the Allies so desperately craved and his place in the history of the Second World War was assured.

Nevertheless, Montgomery could not enjoy his moment of glory for long. With the Torch landings, Montgomery now had to work with his American allies, something that he proved singularly unable to do

LEFT: **Montgomery observes the battlefield from the turret of his command tank.**

with any degree of harmony. He was immediately critical of the manner of the British First Army's approach to Tunisia which in tandem with his own cautious approach, had allowed the remnants of Rommel's army to be reinforced to the tune of 65,000 troops by the end of the year. Moreover, Rommel soon proved that he remained in the game when ignoring Montgomery to his rear, his renamed First Italian Army launched a devastating armoured attack on the US II Corps at the Kasserine Pass. Although his attack soon petered out due to Allied material superiority, Rommel had exposed the inexperience of the American troops and generals. He now attempted to repeat this success against Montgomery, who had been ordered by General Alexander, Deputy Supreme Commander in the Mediterranean, to come to the aid of the Americans at Kasserine. Forewarned of his old adversary's intentions by British intelligence and enjoying a superiority of 400 tanks to Rommel's 142, together with masses of anti-tank guns and artillery, Montgomery succeeded in giving

Rommel 'a bloody nose' at the battle of Medenine on 6 March 1943. Employing the same defensive tactics he had used at Alam Halfa, Montgomery repelled the German's frontal assaults with the loss of one tank to the enemy's fifty. The battle marked the end of Rommel's career in North Africa. Following disagreements with his superiors, he was withdrawn from the theatre, although he would once again cross swords with Montgomery on the beaches of Normandy.

The encounter at Medenine had briefly deflected Montgomery from planning Operation Pugilist, Eighth Army's offensive against the Mareth Line. When this was launched on the 20 March, Montgomery again enjoyed a marked superiority in tanks (743 against 73), anti-tank guns and artillery. Employing a traditional frontal-attack using XXX Corps' infantry, Montgomery hoped to pierce the line near the coast and then use the two armoured divisions of X Corps to

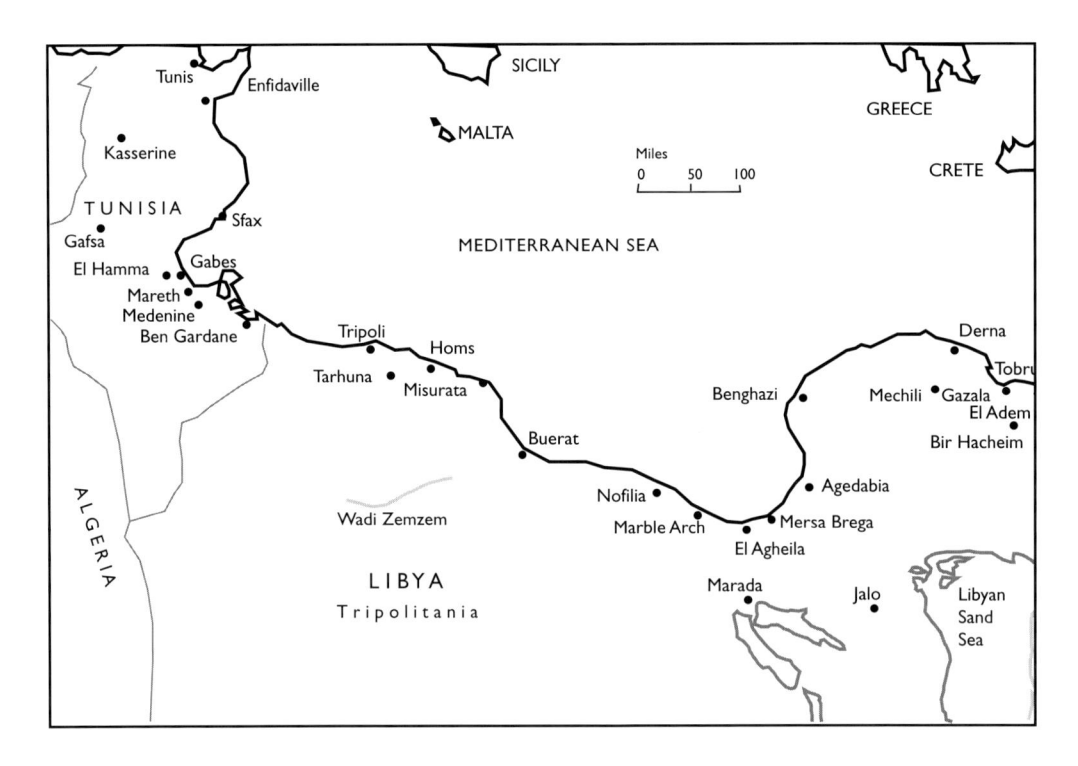

ABOVE: **The Tunisian battlefield.**

RIGHT: **The Lieutenant Governor of Libya, Commander San Marco, surrenders Tripoli to Montgomery at the city's Castel Benito Gate, January 1943.**

break through in the direction of Sfax. In the event, XXX Corps' assault made little progress and their bridgehead was lost during the night of the 22nd. Meantime, Montgomery's flanking attack through the Tebaga Gap, at the western end of the Mareth Line, proved too

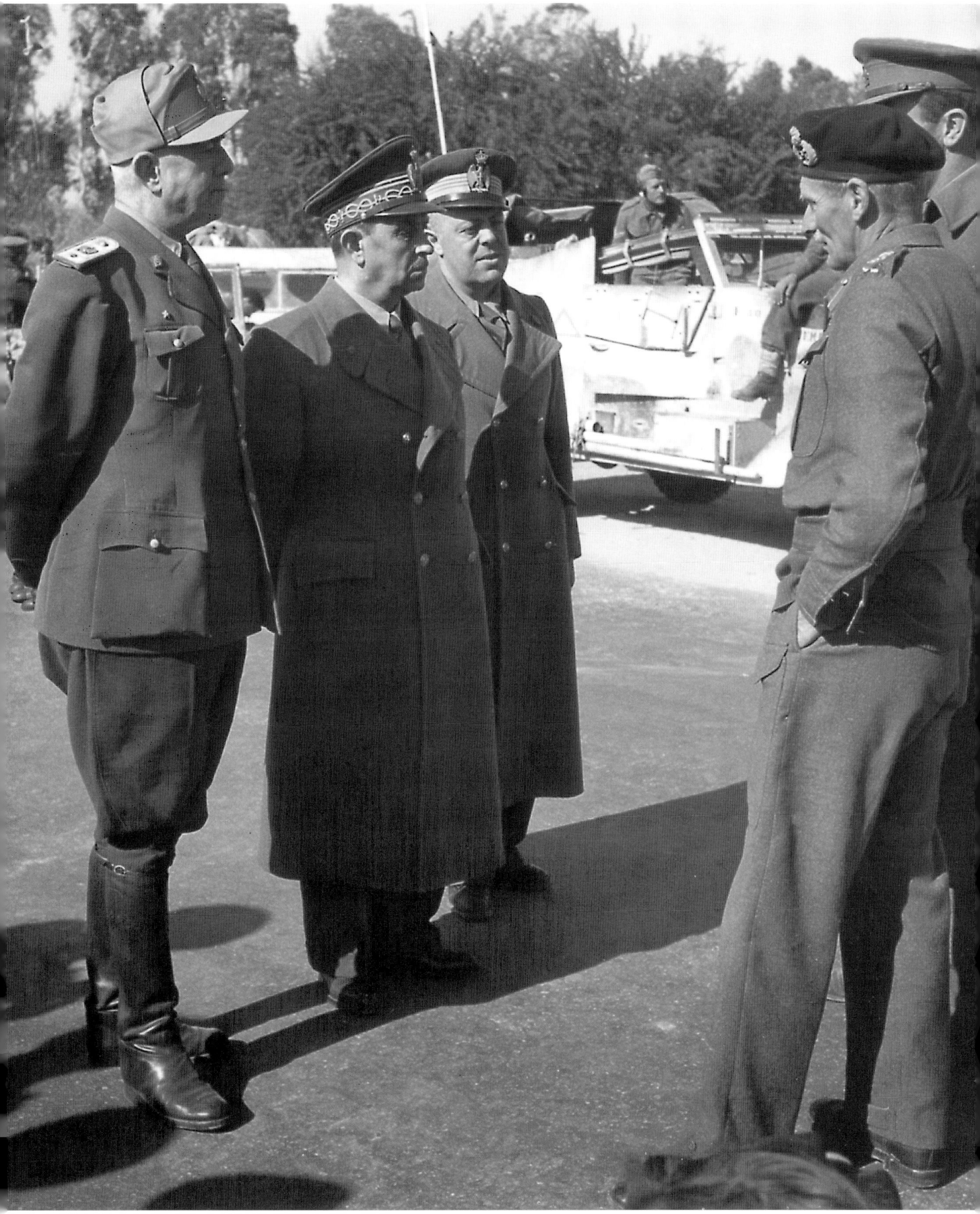

weak and it was only when he switched his main effort there on the 26th, that Eighth Army quickly pushed the enemy back towards El Hamma. Nevertheless, the First Italian Army, now commanded by General Giovanni Messe, was able to establish a new defensive position at Wadi Akarit. Montgomery was, therefore, obliged to pause and prepare another set-piece attack, which in conjunction with First Army, was launched during the early hours of 6 April. Again, however, the attack's initial success was unsatisfactorily exploited and the First Italian Army was able to withdraw in relatively good order to the Enfidaville position.

Nevertheless, the massive material superiority which the Allies had by this time accrued, meant that the final defeat of Axis forces in Tunisia was merely a matter of time. Alexander initially decided that the final drive towards Tunis, codenamed Operation Vulcan, would be entrusted to First Army, with Eighth Army's role being a feint attack on Enfidaville. Under pressure from Montgomery, however, Alexander allowed this attack to become an attempt to break through the line at Enfidaville and to push through into the Cap Bon peninsula. In the event, Montgomery's attack, launched on 19 April in the form of a frontal assault, made such disappointingly slow progress that he was forced to abandon his attack on the 30th and substantially reinforce First Army, whose own attack had also ground to a halt. Using these reinforcements, First Army launched Operation Strike on 6 May which, through sheer weight of numbers, saw Tunis fall on 7 May and all enemy resistance cease six days later. The victory was marked by a cable from Alexander to Churchill which simply stated: 'Sir, it is my duty to report that the Tunisian campaign is over. All enemy resistance has ceased. We are masters of the North African shores.' Montgomery, meanwhile, invited Field Marshal

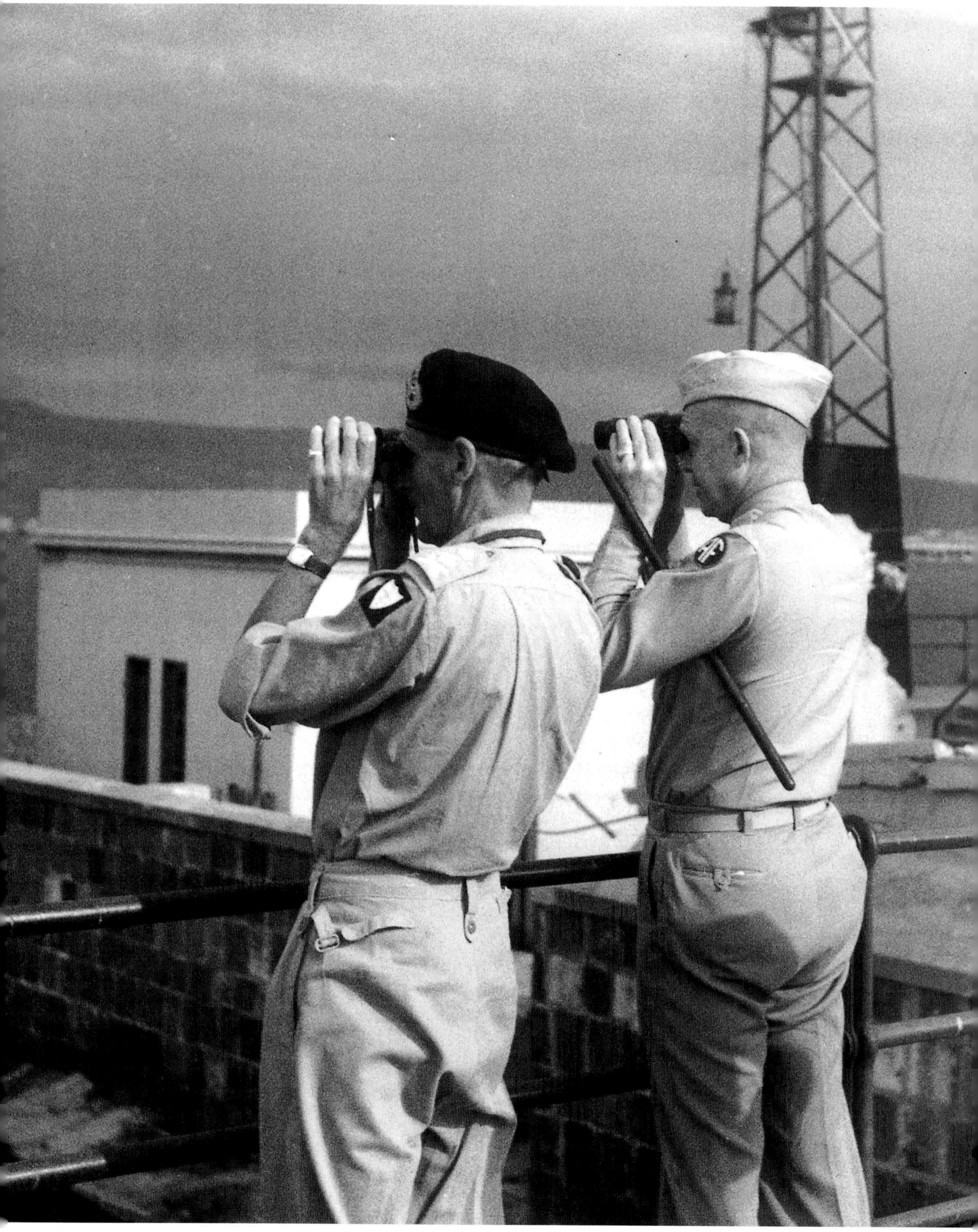

Messe, defeated commander of the Italian First Army, to dinner, over which the recent campaign was discussed.

The whole Tunisian campaign was fought out against a background of confused and often bitter discussion surrounding planning for the invasion of Sicily, codenamed Operation Husky and the next logical step in the Mediterranean war. These tensions were largely precipitated by Montgomery. From the moment Alexander invited him to participate in the preparations for Husky in February 1943, Montgomery paid scant regard to the need for cordial Alliance relations and instead seemed to go out of his way to offend his American counterparts, particularly General Dwight Eisenhower, the

LEFT: **General Eisenhower and Montgomery view the Italian mainland from Messina, Sicily, September 1943.**

OVERLEAF: **Montgomery congratulates the officers and men of Eighth Army and presents awards won during the campaign in Sicily.**

IGNEM VEN

TTERE IN TERRAM

Supreme Commander of all Allied forces in the Mediterranean. For example, by capturing Sfax by 10 April, Montgomery had won a bet with Eisenhower and demanded no less than his own Flying Fortress as payment. Montgomery's complete lack of tact when dealing with his new allies was born out of his distrust of the American's fighting qualities, especially after the disaster at the Kasserine Pass. Concerning Eisenhower, Montgomery declared that 'he was good probably on the political line; but he obviously knows nothing whatever about fighting', while American soldiers would not fight because 'they haven't got the light of battle in their eyes' and lacked confidence in their generals. For their part, Montgomery's American colleagues soon became increasingly irritated by what they saw as his, at times, unnecessary caution. Montgomery's views on the Americans were, however, shared by Alexander and were to have a profound influence on the planning and conduct of Husky.

Montgomery soon declared the existing plan, which involved multiple but isolated landings around the island, as a recipe for disaster, arguing that the Tunisian experience had shown that Allied attacks had only succeeded through an overwhelming concentration of force. By dispersing their effort in Sicily, the Allies would openly invite defeat by the vastly more experienced German units that would undoubtedly reinforce the island. Threatening resignation if his own plan, which envisaged concentrated landings in the south of the island, was not accepted, Montgomery finally got his way on 3 May 1943. However, his subsequent demand that the US Seventh Army, commanded by Lieutenant-General George S. Patton, be placed directly under his command for the invasion was refused,

OVERLEAF: **Montgomery reading a poster from Welsh miners who had sent a message to Eighth Army, November 1943. The poster pledges their full support for the forces in Italy and guarantees them sufficient supplies of coal.**

SOUTH WALES MINERS' MESSAGE

"SOUTH WALES MINERS CONGRATULATE HEROIC EFFORTS of ALLIED ARMIES NOW FIGHTING VALIANTLY ON BEHALF OF BRITISH PEOPLE ON ITALIAN SOIL. WE AWAIT FURTHER DEVELOPMENTS WITH FAITH IN YOUR DETERMINATION AND ABILITY TO ACHIEVE ALL YOUR OBJECTIVES. WE PLEDGE FULL SUPPORT OF MINEWORKERS OF THIS GREAT COALFIELD and GUARANTEE SUFFICIENT COAL TO MAINTAIN SUPPLIES TO MEET ALL THE NEEDS OF YOUR FORCES."

GENERAL MONTGOMERY'S REPLY

"PLEASE GIVE MY BEST WISHES TO ALL SOUTH WALES MINERS and TELL THEM THAT IF THEY WILL PRODUCE THE COAL WE WILL FINISH THE JOB HERE ON THE BATTLEFRONT. ALL MY TROOPS ARE IN VERY GOOD SPIRITS."

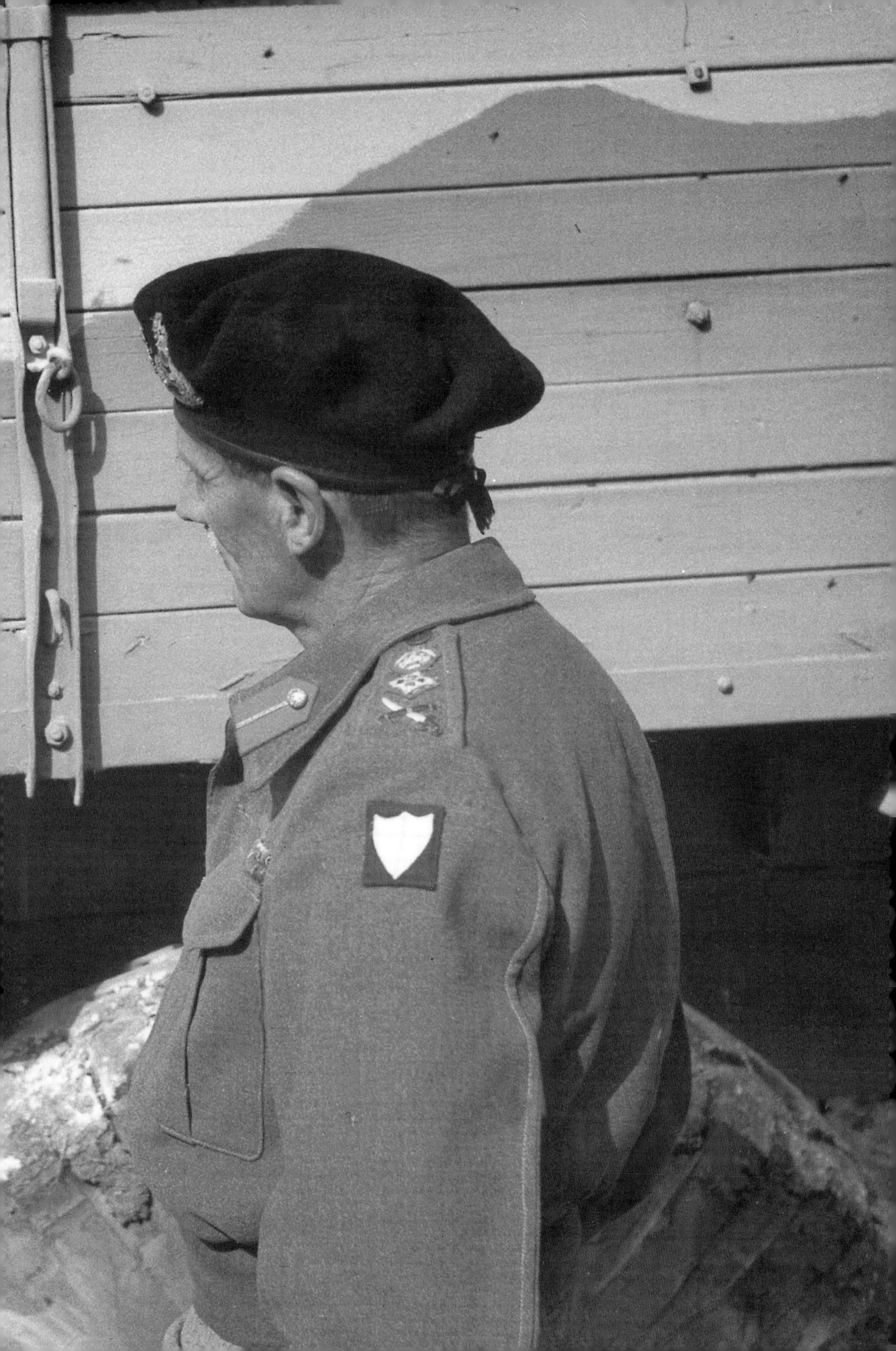

causing him to write scornfully in his diary that 'political reasons' had forced a compromise 'opposed to all sound military common sense'.

Before Husky was launched, however, Montgomery requested a period of leave, citing exhaustion from fighting 'to keep our own show from going off the rails'. Returning to England for the first time since his victory at El Alamein, Montgomery was delighted to discover that he had become a national celebrity. Nevertheless, upon his return to North Africa on 2 June, he received a severe dressing down from Brooke over the Flying Fortress affair and Montgomery was made all too aware that he was part of a coalition now, whether he liked it or not. Montgomery certainly did not like, and his inability to keep these feelings suppressed became all too apparent during the Sicilian campaign, which commenced on 10 July 1943.

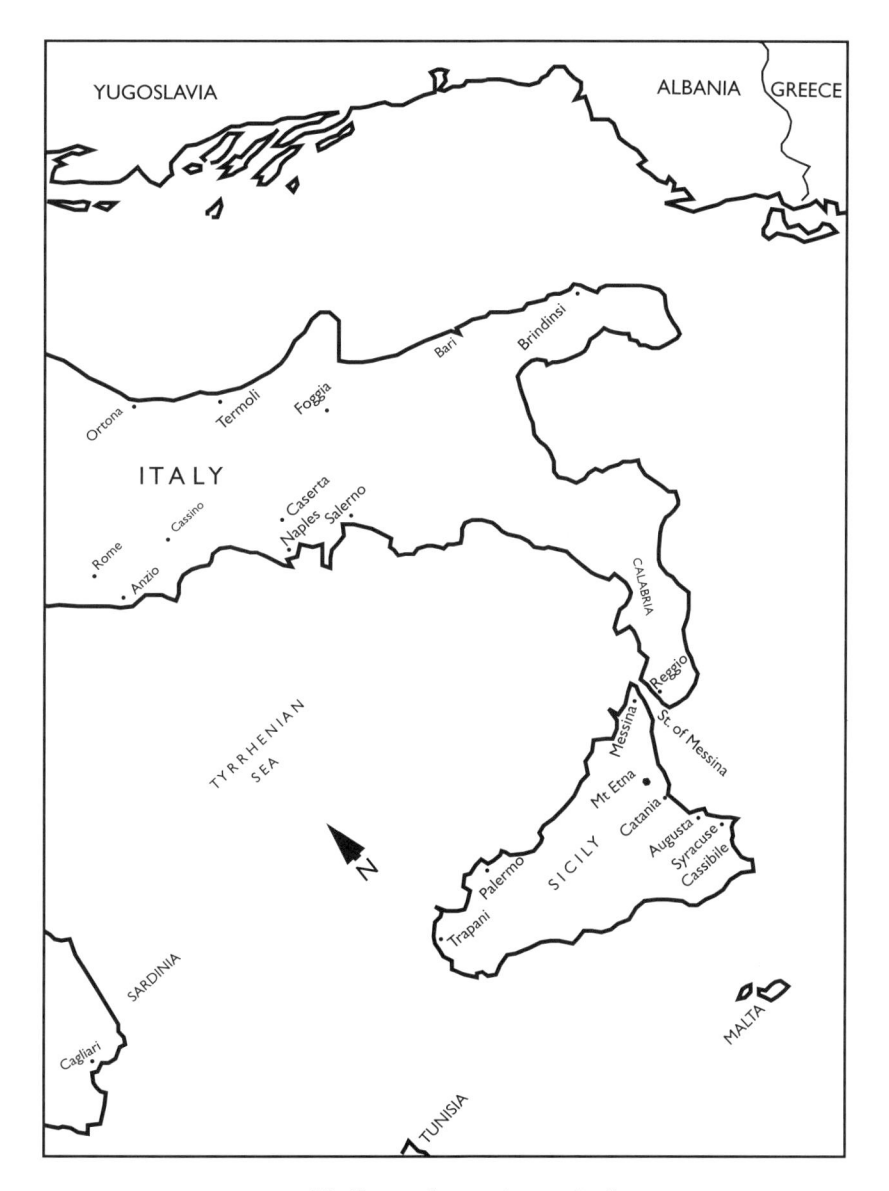

ABOVE: **Sicily and southern Italy.**

OVERLEAF: **Montgomery having tea in a Sicilian orchard, September 1943.**

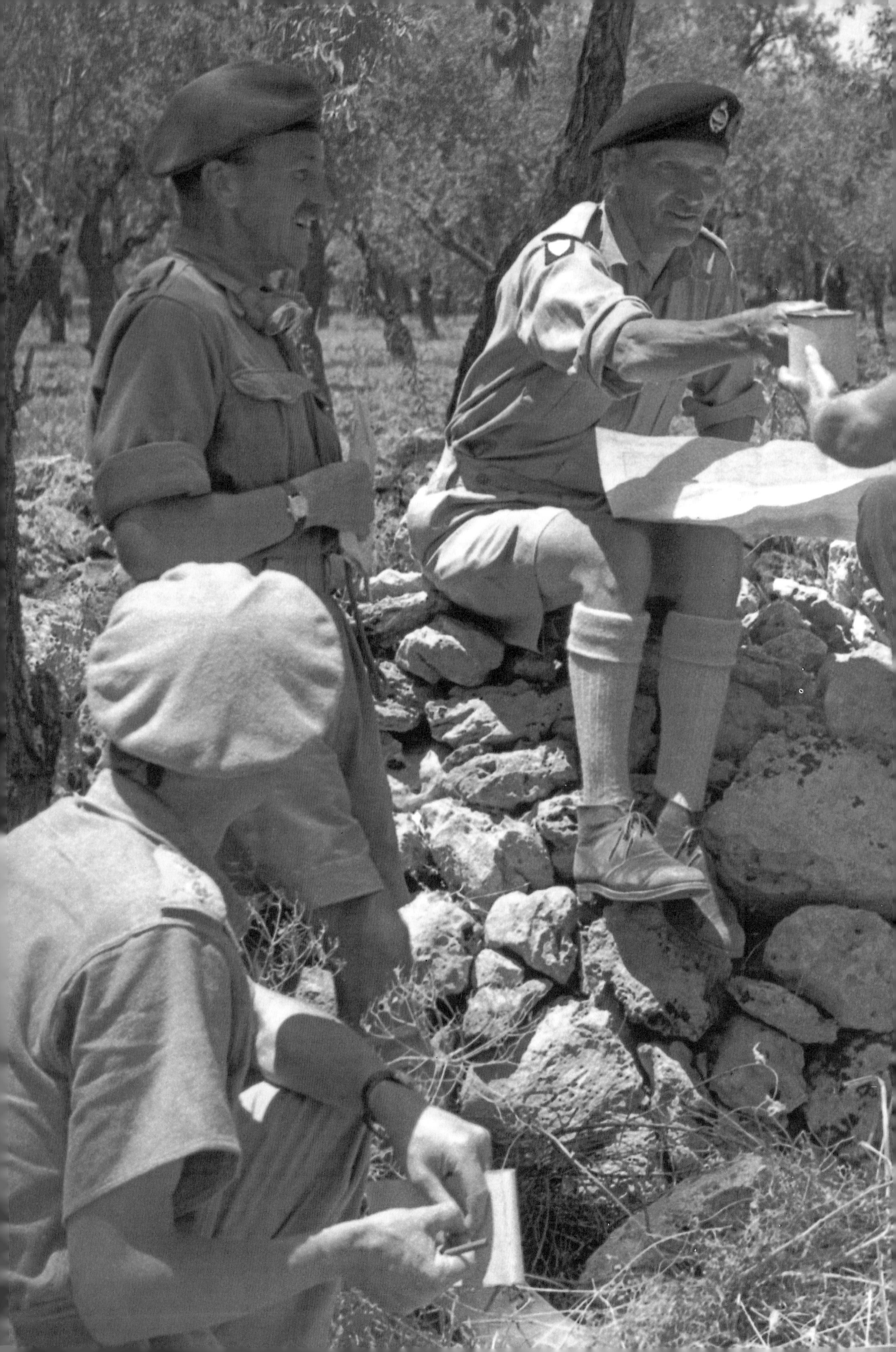

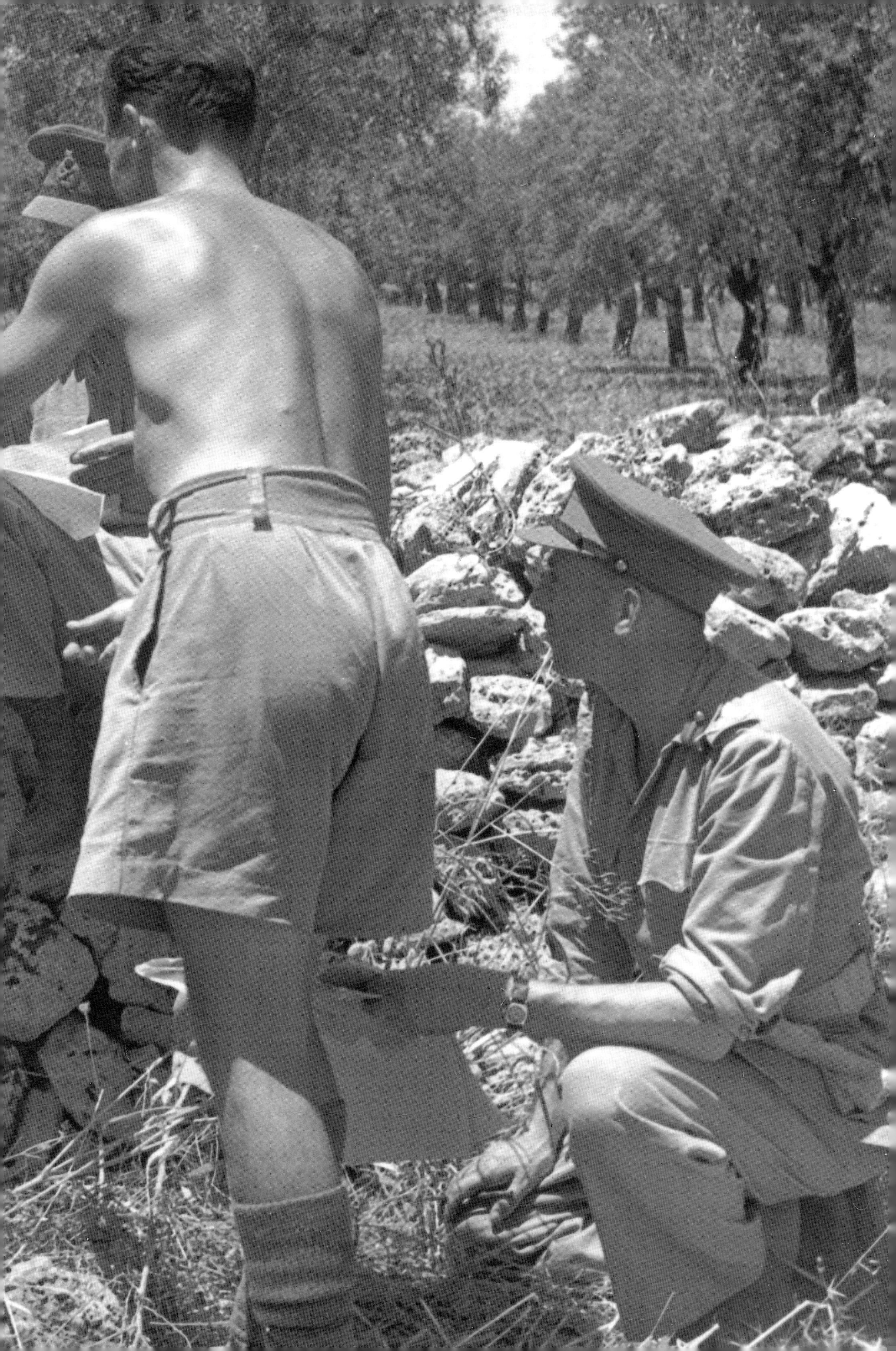

Despite his reservations concerning the initial amphibious phase of Husky, Montgomery appeared vindicated when his revised plan proved triumphant. Although the parachute landings foundered in the sea, both Patton's Seventh Army and Eighth Army landed successfully, the latter on the south-eastern coast between Syracuse and Cape Passero. Eighth Army's ultimate objective was Messina and buoyed by his initial success, Montgomery ordered his XXX Corps to push inland, while XIII Corps was to advance up the coast towards Catania. However, the Germans had established an effective defence in the mountainous terrain north of Catania and a savage five day battle ensued. By 19 July, Montgomery conceded that the capture of Catania and an advance along the undefended coast road to Messina was now unattainable. Instead, he begged Alexander to order Patton to act as his flank guard while he switched his main effort to the north-west, where XXX Corps was ordered to pierce the newly formed Etna Line and perform a 'left hook' around Mount Etna to the coast below Messina. Alexander duly obliged, but Patton was so annoyed at Montgomery's arrogance that he instead gained permission from Alexander to carry out a wholly unnecessary diversion to capture Palermo, which he achieved on 22 July. Moreover, by splitting Eighth Army's attack into two separate thrusts, Montgomery had allowed the Germans to successfully defend against both. The ensuing stalemate obliged Montgomery to ask Patton to execute a northern thrust from Palermo towards Messina and the latter triumphantly entered Messina three weeks later on 17 August, thus bringing the Sicilian campaign to a close.

OVERLEAF: **Monty's Mascots. Montgomery with a cage of birds bearing the Eighth Army crest, outside his mobile caravan in Italy, December 1943. During quiet moments, Montgomery often enjoyed the company of canaries from Sicily and Italian love-birds.**

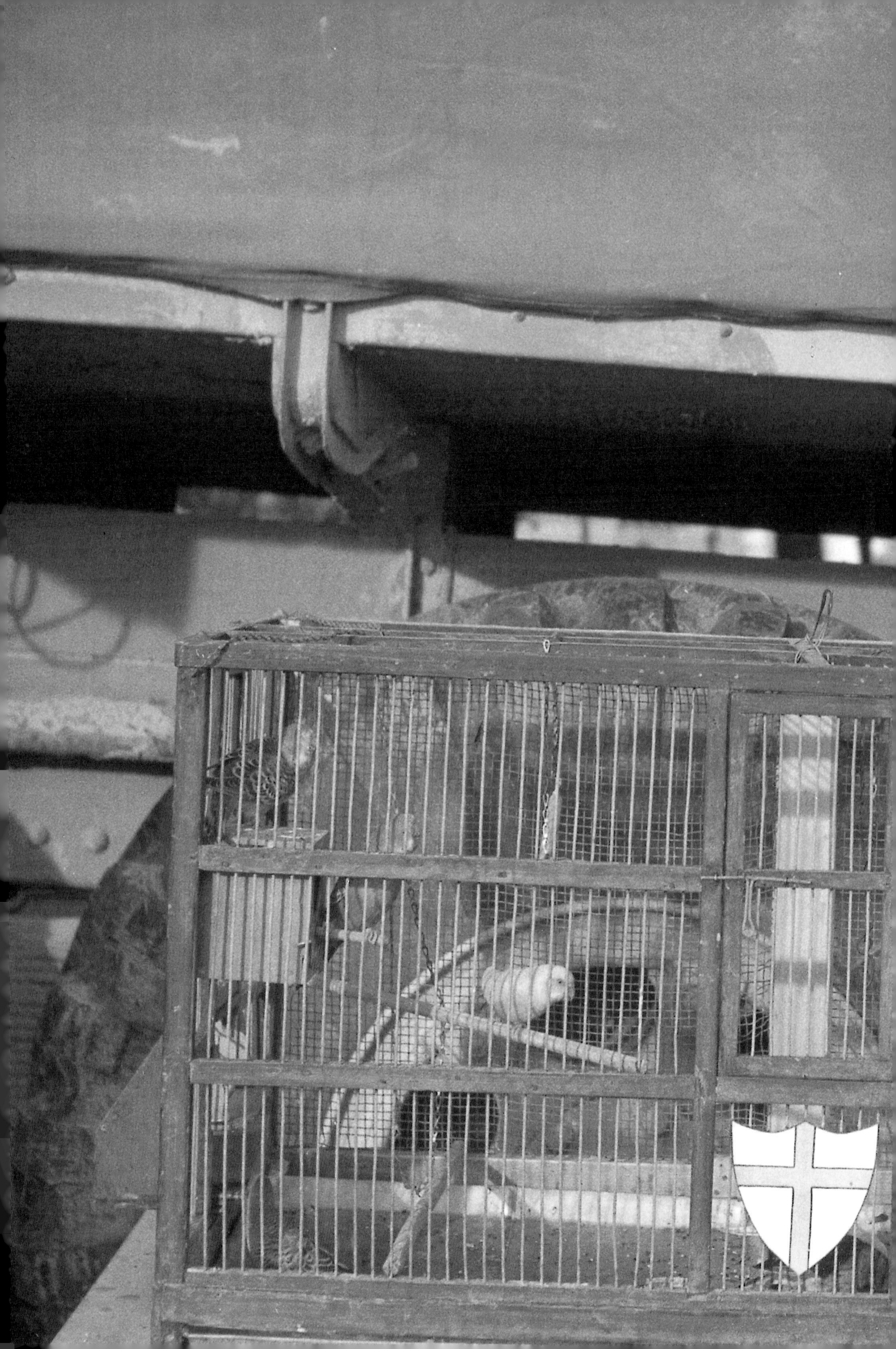

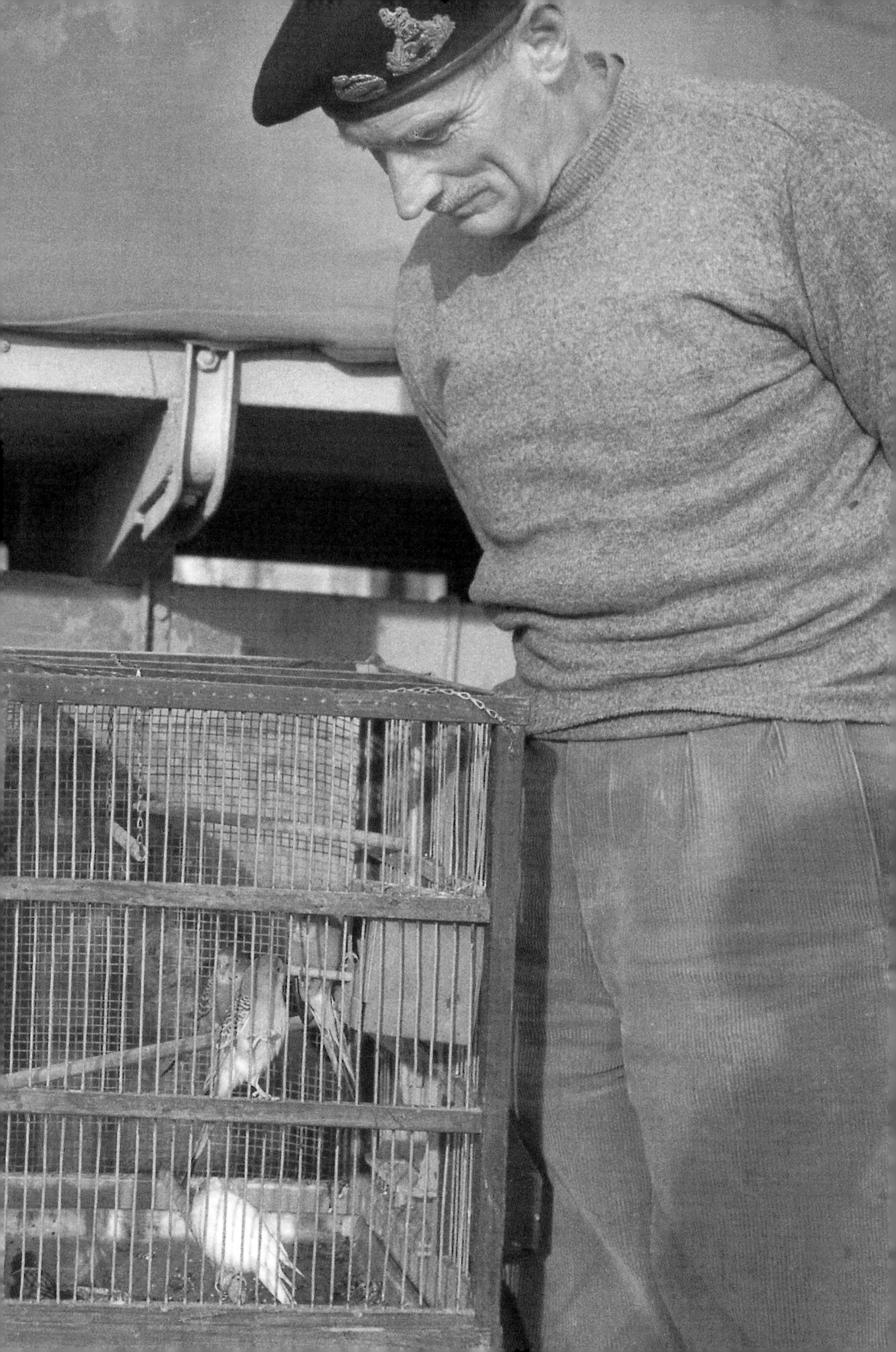

Any thought of celebration was negated by the fact that large amounts of German troops and equipment had been allowed to escape to the Italian mainland and that the whole campaign had degenerated into 'a horse race' towards Messina, as Patton himself declared. Indeed, Patton's extremely vain behaviour throughout the campaign – such as having his entrance into Messina specially filmed – led Montgomery to suggest that public relations were taking precedence over military professionalism and that soldiers' lives would be squandered as a result.

Montgomery's frustration, particularly with the higher direction of the war, became all too apparent during the lull between the conquest of Sicily and the invasion of the Italian mainland. Once again, he expressed extreme misgivings over the proposed plan for the invasion and the resources allocated to it. Most of these were directed against Eisenhower, whom he felt was concentrating too much attention on the political aspect of the campaign (namely the surrender of Italian troops), and too little on the military problems of conducting an invasion against determined German resistance in a country whose climate and terrain were ideally suited to defence. Much of Montgomery's carping however, resulted from the fact that he was denied his expected command of the main assault. Code-named Operation Avalanche, this was instead entrusted to the US Fifth Army under the command of Lieutenant-General Mark Clark, who was to execute an amphibious landing at Salerno in the Bay of Naples. Montgomery was given the purely subsidiary role of landing

OVERLEAF: **General Montgomery leaving his forward headquarters in an amphibious 'duck' on his way to greet Lieutenant-General Mark Clark, commander of the US Fifth Army at Salerno.**

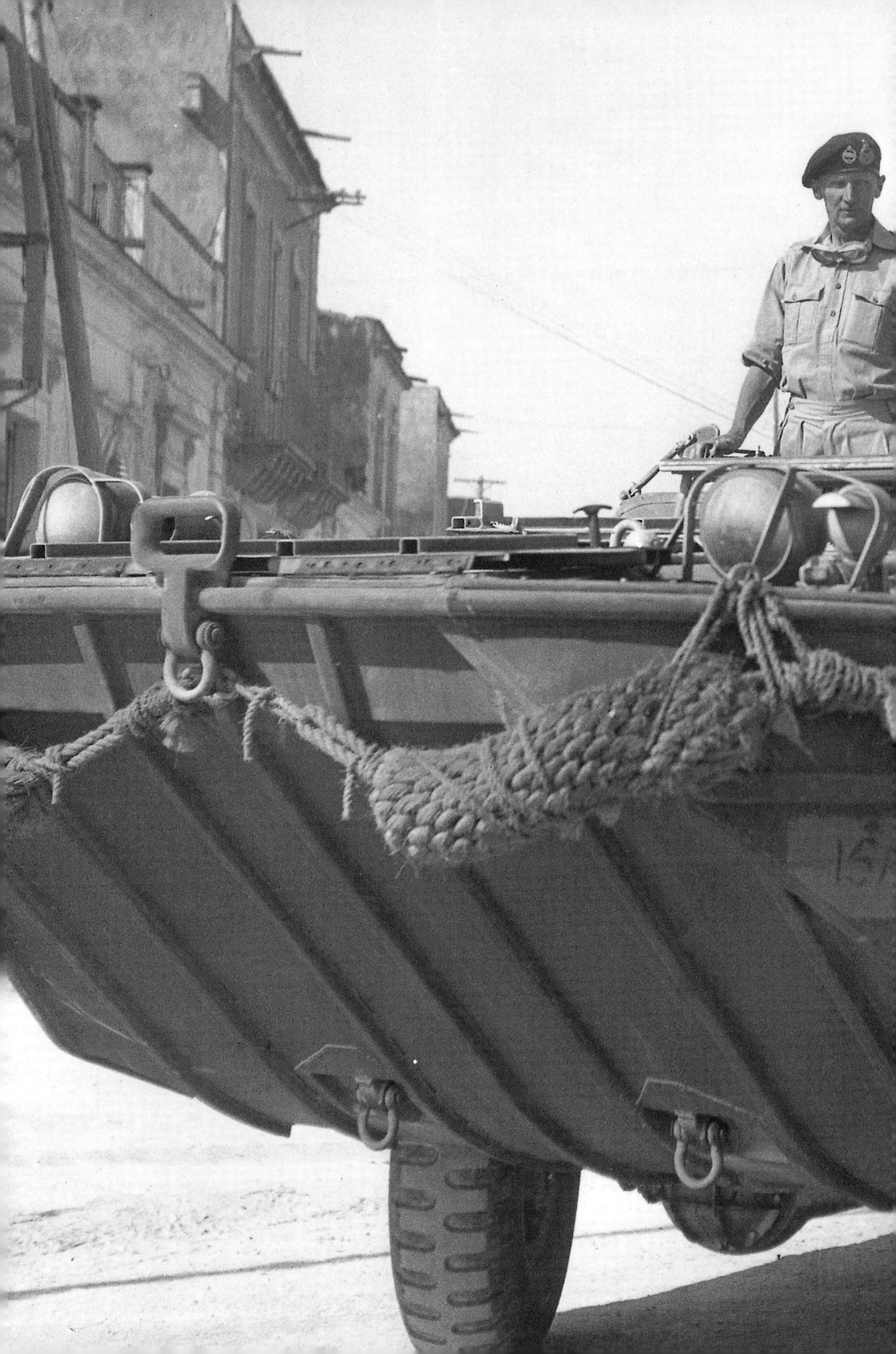

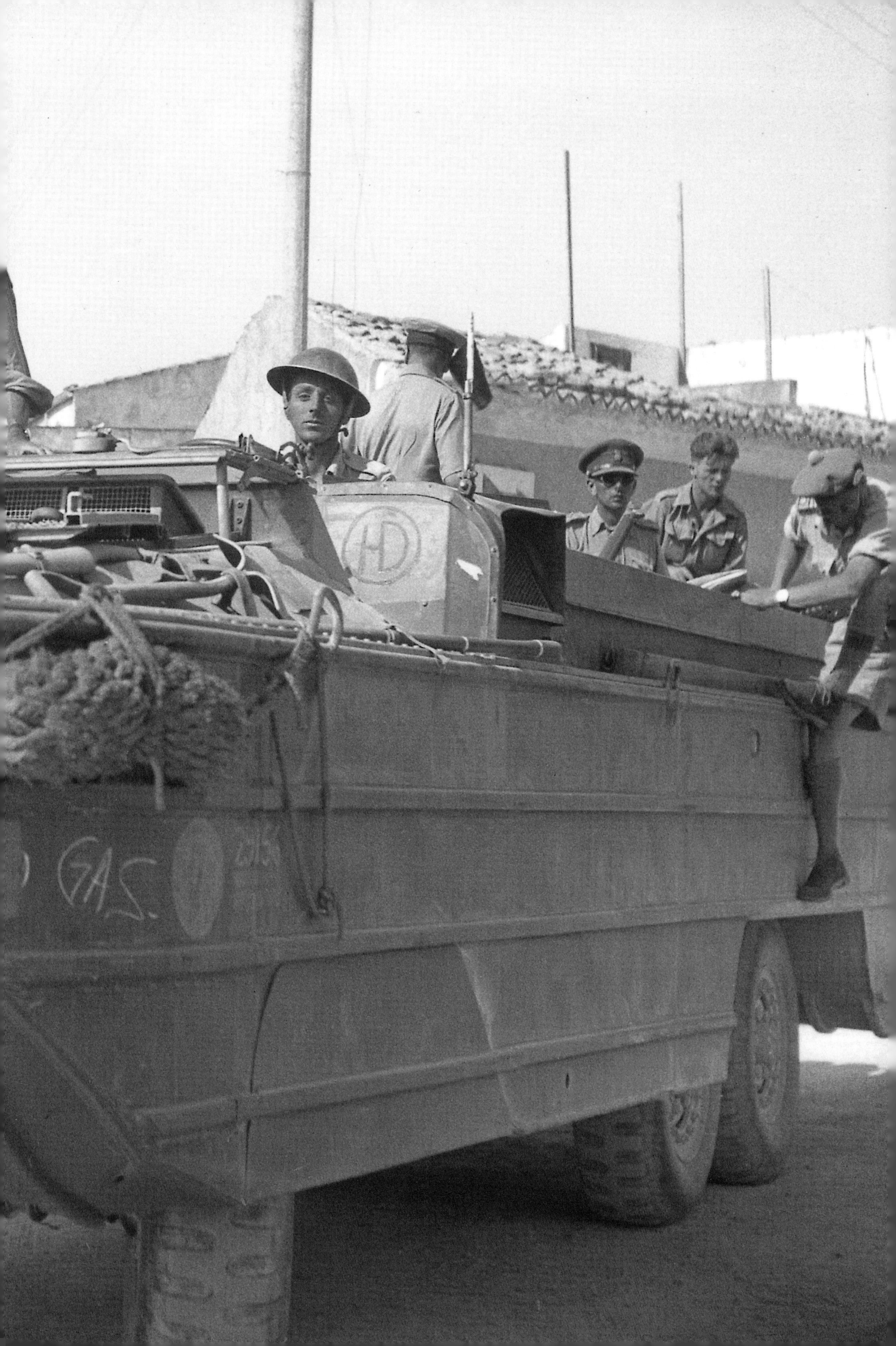
GAS

Eighth Army at Reggio, directly across the Strait of Messina on the 'toe' of Italy. Preceded by a massive artillery bombardment, Montgomery achieved this on 3 September 1943, only to discover that the Germans had already withdrawn from the area and established defensive positions amidst the mountainous country of central Calabria. Consequently, Montgomery advanced with a great degree of ease over the next five days and pushed some 100 miles northwards into southern Italy.

By contrast, however, while further elements of Eighth Army were landed further to the east on the 'heel' of Italy in Operation Slapstick, Avalanche, launched on 9 September, soon found itself faced with possible disaster. Montgomery had warned Alexander the previous day that the Salerno landings might be rapidly contained by the German Tenth Army, and so it proved. Fierce German counter-attacks quickly threatened the fragile beachhead and Alexander frantically urged Montgomery to come to Clark's aid. Montgomery still harboured resentment at being denied Clark's job and therefore failed to show any urgency in his push northwards, arguing that Fifth Army was alone responsible for extricating itself from a mess of its own making. In the event, Fifth Army did prevail at Salerno and captured Naples on 1 October, although at the time, Montgomery ironically claimed that Eighth Army's arrival had precipitated the German withdrawal to the heavily defended Gustav Line, centred on the town of Cassino.

Following the capture of Auletta and Potenza and the link-up with Fifth Army in mid-September, Montgomery was ordered to join up with the Slapstick forces, which were advancing on Foggia, and progress along the Adriatic coast of Italy towards the River Sangro, just to the south of the Gustav Line. Frustrated though he was with the lack of direction from above, Montgomery dutifully fought his way northwards along the Adriatic coast. But in the face of determined German resistance over terrain that was ideally suited to defensive action, the progress of Eighth Army was extremely slow. Furthermore, its fighting effectiveness was by now severely impaired both by almost continual fighting since El Alamein and by manpower shortages due to the withdrawal of forces for the invasion of France. Although Foggia was taken with little fighting on 27 September and the whole of the Gargano peninsula cleared by 1 October, Montgomery's progress was soon checked by the Bernhard Line (so named because its aim was to stop Montgomery) which straddled the Volturno and Biferno rivers. Having learnt that the Germans were preparing to defend Termoli, situated just behind the Biferno, Montgomery planned an audacious amphibious commando raid to capture the town. Comprising over a thousand men, this was launched on 20 October and, after an unopposed landing to the north of the town, Termoli was quickly taken from the stunned Germans. The bridgehead was quickly counter-attacked, however, by the 16th Panzer Division and the town was only secured after a desperate and bloody battle. Following Termoli, the Germans withdrew to the River Trigno, and the airfields at Foggia, now safe from enemy counter-attack, became fully operational.

Despite his success at Termoli, Montgomery's mood remained grim. He continued to complain about his supply situation and the higher direction of the campaign, which had resulted in the prestige prize of Rome being assigned to Clark while he was left with the unglamorous push up the Adriatic coast. After heavy fighting on the

OVERLEAF: **Montgomery with General Sir Alan Brooke.**

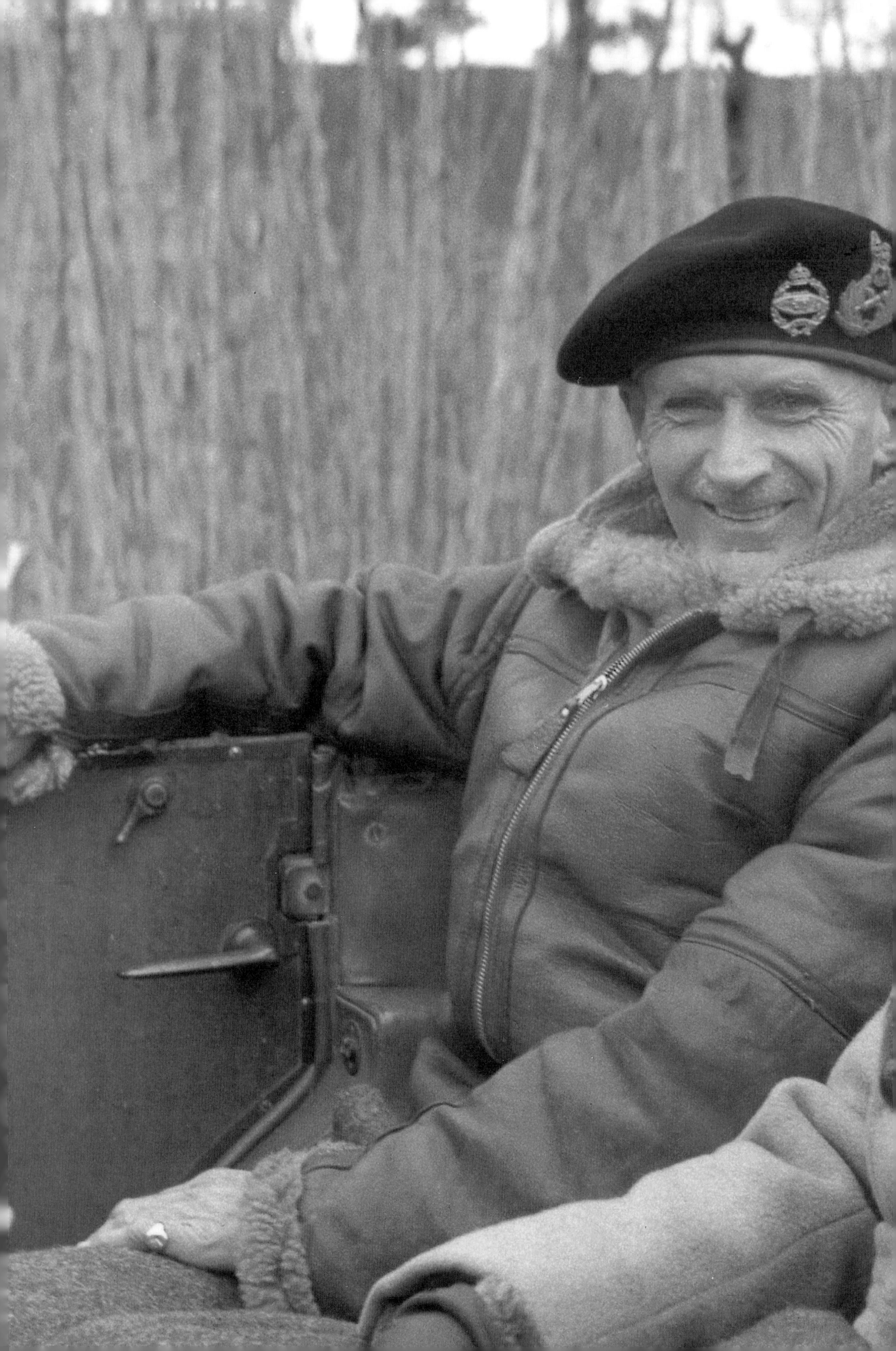

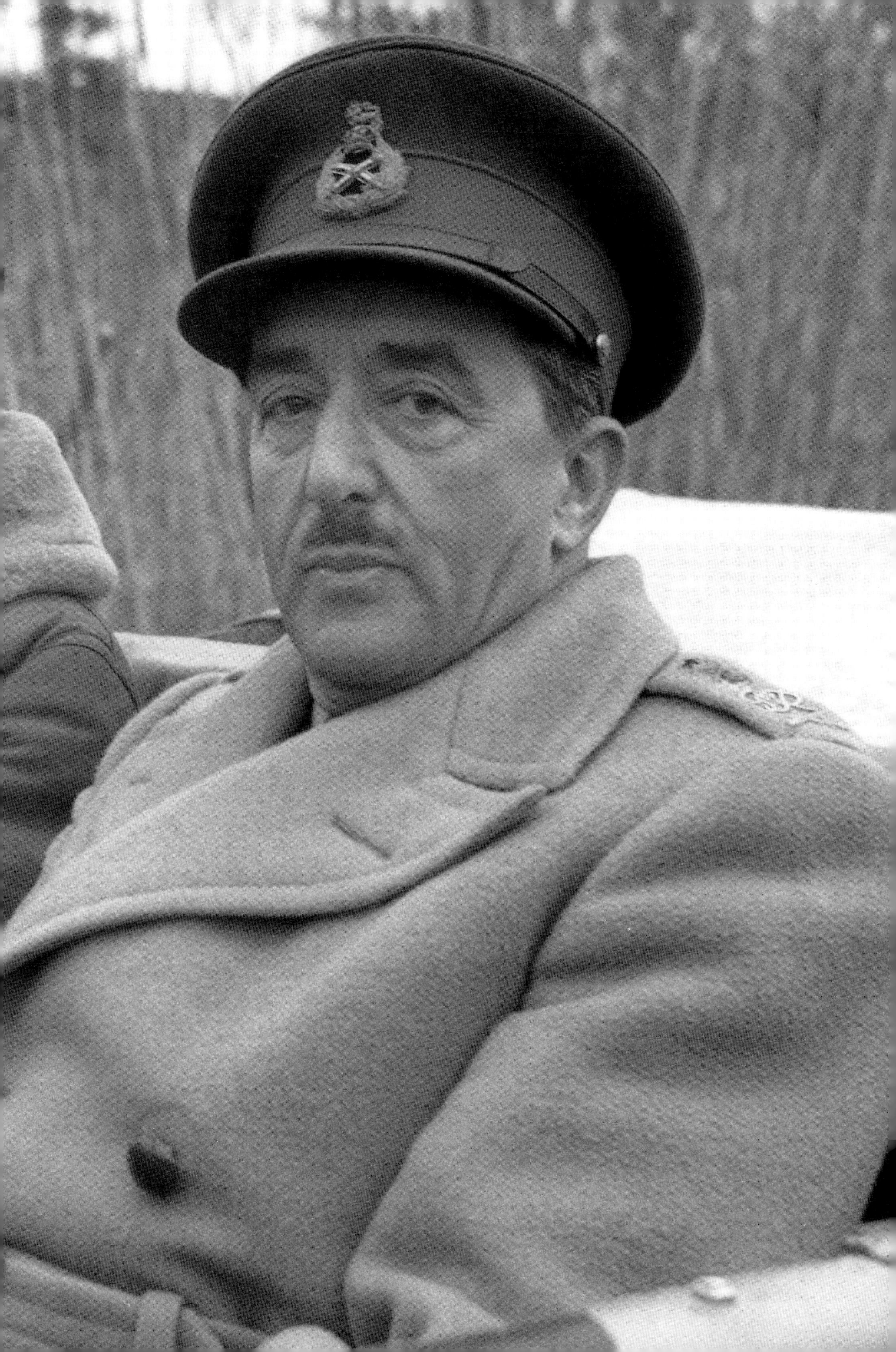

Trigno at the start of November, Montgomery's negative frame of mind was deepened when the weather broke. Torrential and incessant rain quickly immobilized his armour and grounded his air support, effectively ending his fleeting hopes of out-flanking the Gustav Line and capturing Rome from the east, ahead of Clark. Nevertheless, by mid-November, Montgomery had reached the banks of the Sangro and thus faced the formidable Gustav Line. The Sangro was a daunting obstacle, 400 feet wide and dominated by high ground on the far side. Under the cover of a heavy artillery barrage, Montgomery attempted to secure this high ground by sneaking across enough light forces to secure a bridgehead. After particularly heavy fighting, a slender lodgement had been secured by 27 November and over the next few days, Montgomery launched a concerted assault to seize the high ground while the weather was fine. By 1 December, 1,000 Germans had been taken prisoner but, despite his assertion that 'my troops have won the battle as they always do...the road to Rome is open', Montgomery had merely dented the Gustav Line. Any chance of breaching it was lost when in the face of concerted German counter-attacks, more heavy rain over 4-5 December caused the Sangro to burst its banks and sever all communication across the river. Accordingly, when Brooke visited him on 14 December, Montgomery conceded that there was little hope of capturing Rome before the following spring, especially in view of the inept way he believed Clark was handling Fifth Army. Instead, Montgomery felt that the Italian front should remain dormant for the rest of the winter and he set about securing a defensive line through the newly captured towns of Orsogna and Ortona.

During his visit, Brooke had noted that Montgomery was 'looking tired and definitely wants a rest and a change'. Throughout the Sicilian and Italian campaigns, the 'change' on which Montgomery had set his heart, was to be assigned a prominent role in the cross-Channel invasion. Throughout the summer and autumn, he had regularly written to Brooke and his friend 'Simbo' Simpson at the War Office with suggestions as to how Operation Overlord should be conducted, including hints concerning the part he could play in it. After lengthy deliberation and much to Montgomery's 'relief and excitement', he received confirmation on 24 December 1943, that he was to assume command of 21st Army Group for Overlord. Although he bid an emotional farewell to his beloved Eighth Army on 30 December – his Farewell Message stated that 'It is difficult to express to you adequately what this parting means to me' – Montgomery wrote of his Overlord assignment that it would be 'the biggest thing I have ever had to handle' and was convinced it would be the decisive campaign of the war.

RIGHT: **Canadian troops cheer as Montgomery tells them of Mussolini's resignation during the campaign in Sicily, 25 July 1943.**

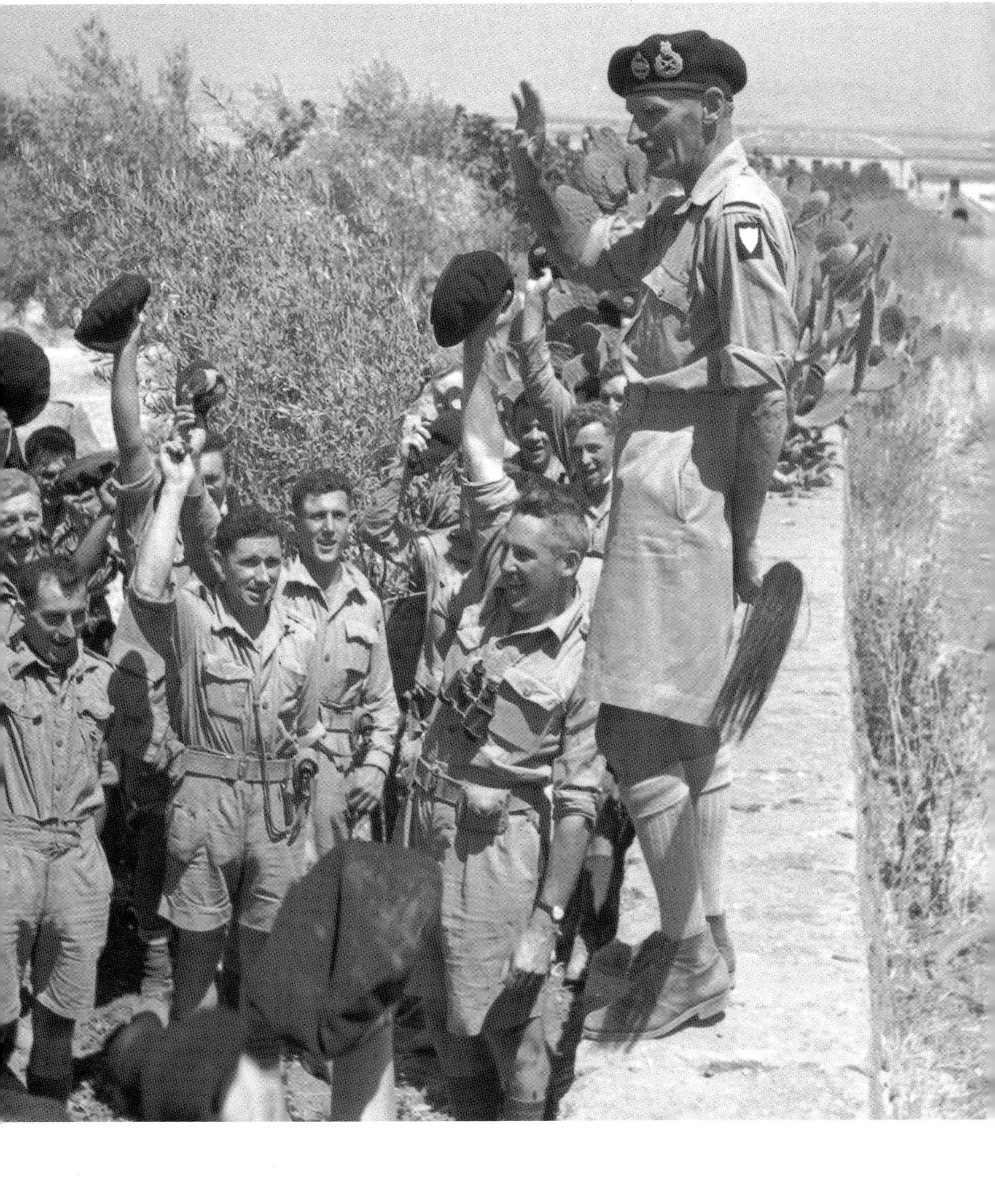

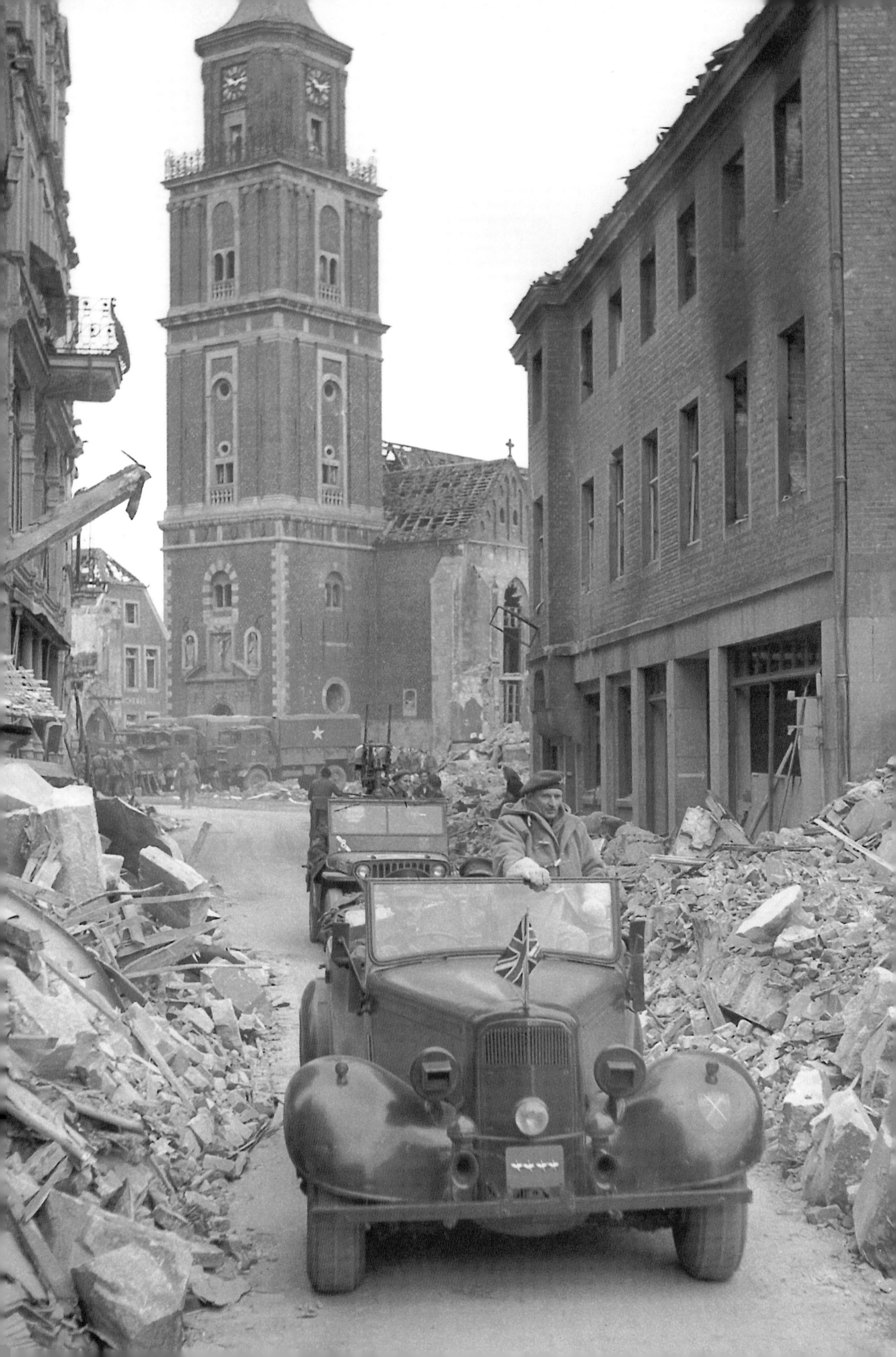

CHAPTER 4

D-DAY AND THE BATTLE OF NORMANDY

MONTGOMERY'S APPOINTMENT placed him in sole charge of all land forces, including the Canadians and Americans, for the initial landing phase of Overlord, which was to take place in Normandy, France. Almost immediately, Montgomery criticized the existing draft plan for the invasion, codenamed Cossac, which he felt could only lead to disaster. Its limited strength of only three divisions along narrow beachheads would allow the Germans to isolate and destroy

LEFT: **Montgomery advances through a heavily damaged town during the campaign in north-west Europe.**

them. With the agreement of Eisenhower, who had been named Supreme Commander for Overlord, Montgomery succeeded in two respects: firstly he deferred D-Day from May to early June 1944 so that more landing-craft which were in very short supply could be produced; secondly he increased the initial assault force to five divisions, backed up by three airborne divisions which would simultaneously be dropped inland. Montgomery was also responsible for persuading a reluctant Churchill to divert resources from the strategic bombing campaign against Germany into conducting a preliminary air offensive against the French rail and road system leading to Normandy, thus delaying German

RIGHT: **Montgomery greets General De Gaulle upon his arrival in France, 14 June 1944, stepping on French soil for the first time since the German occupation of his country.**

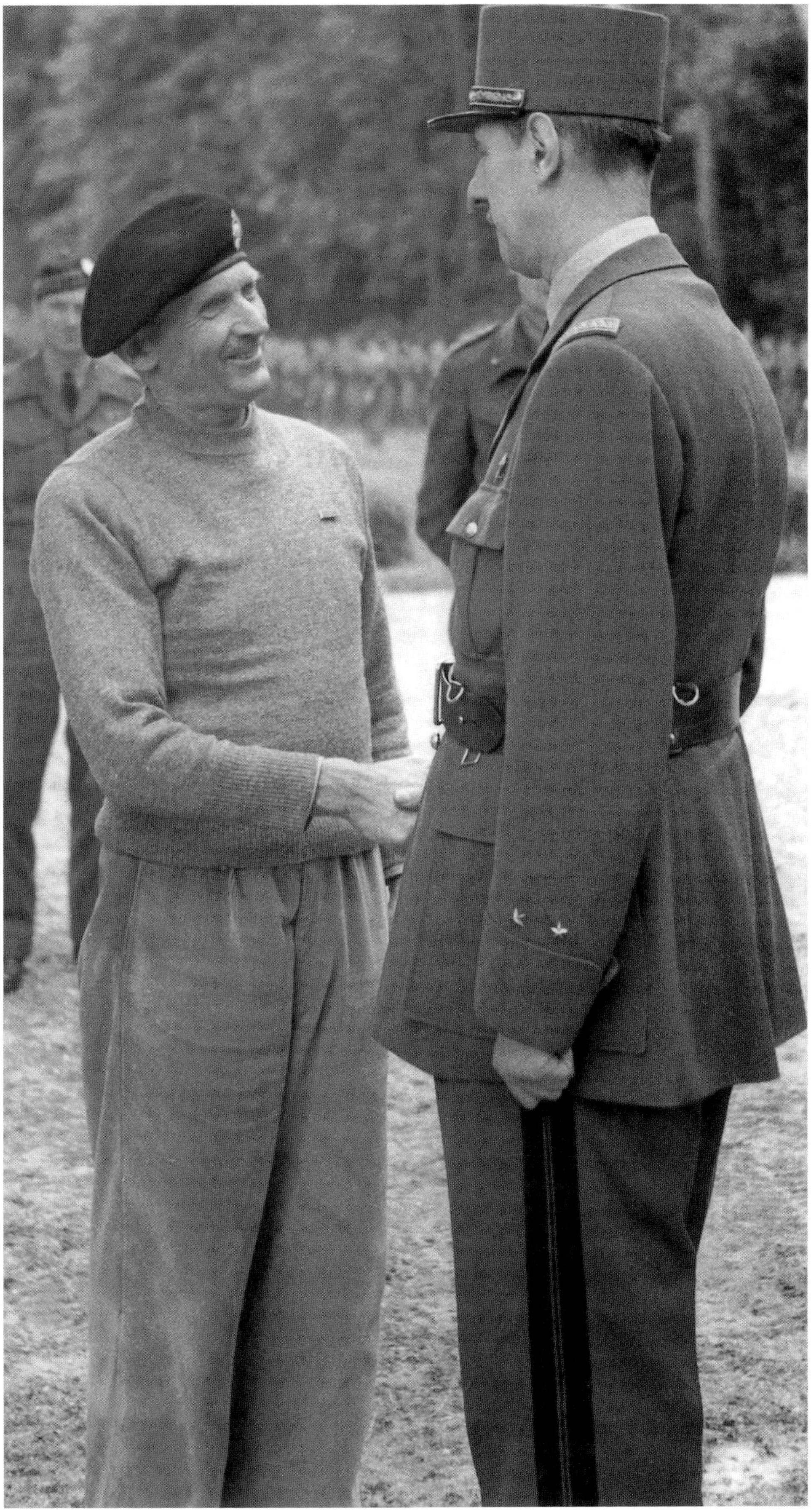

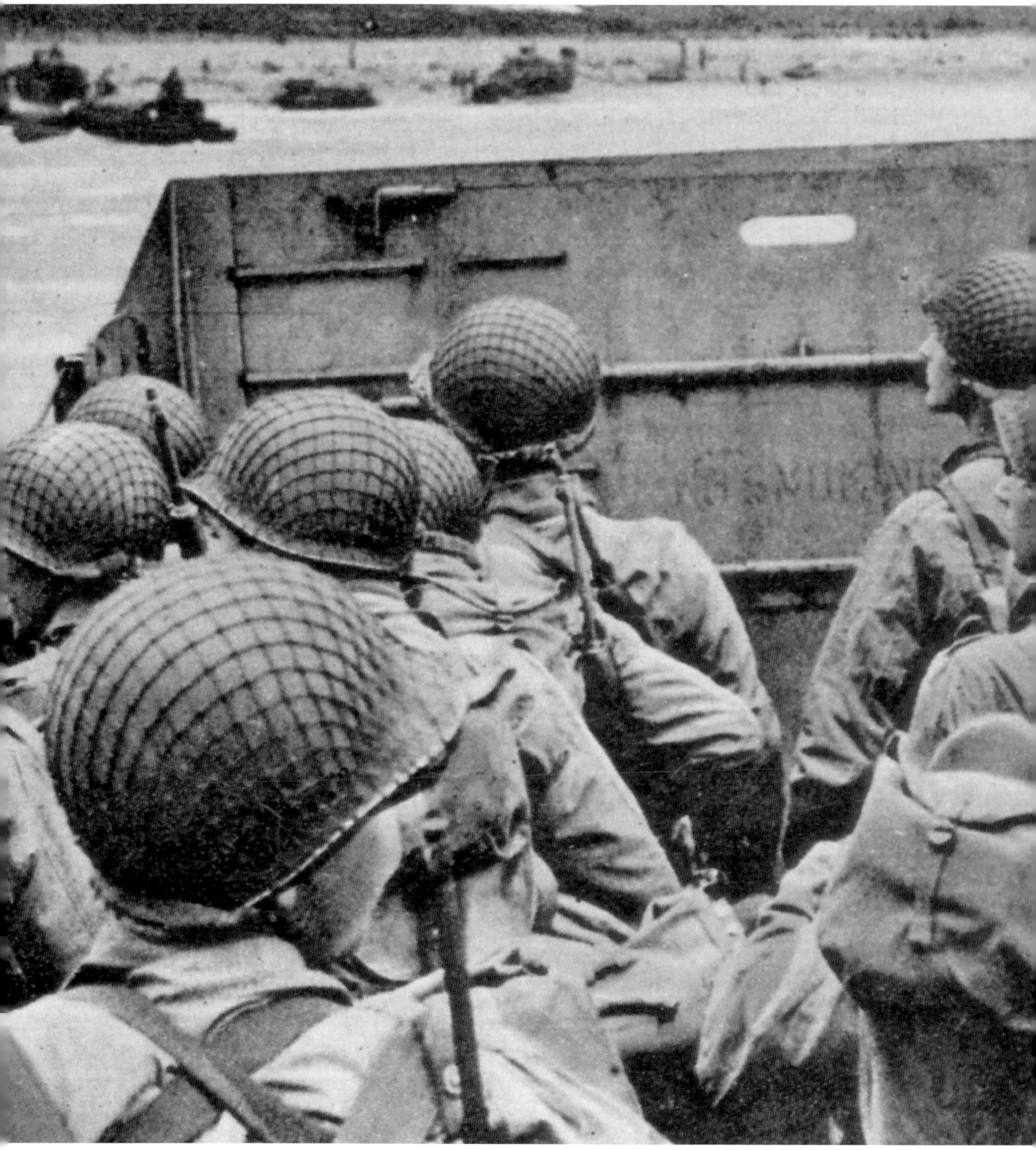

LEFT: **American troops prepare to land on the shores of Normandy.**

OVERLEAF: **From left to right: Brooke, Churchill, Patton and Montgomery.**

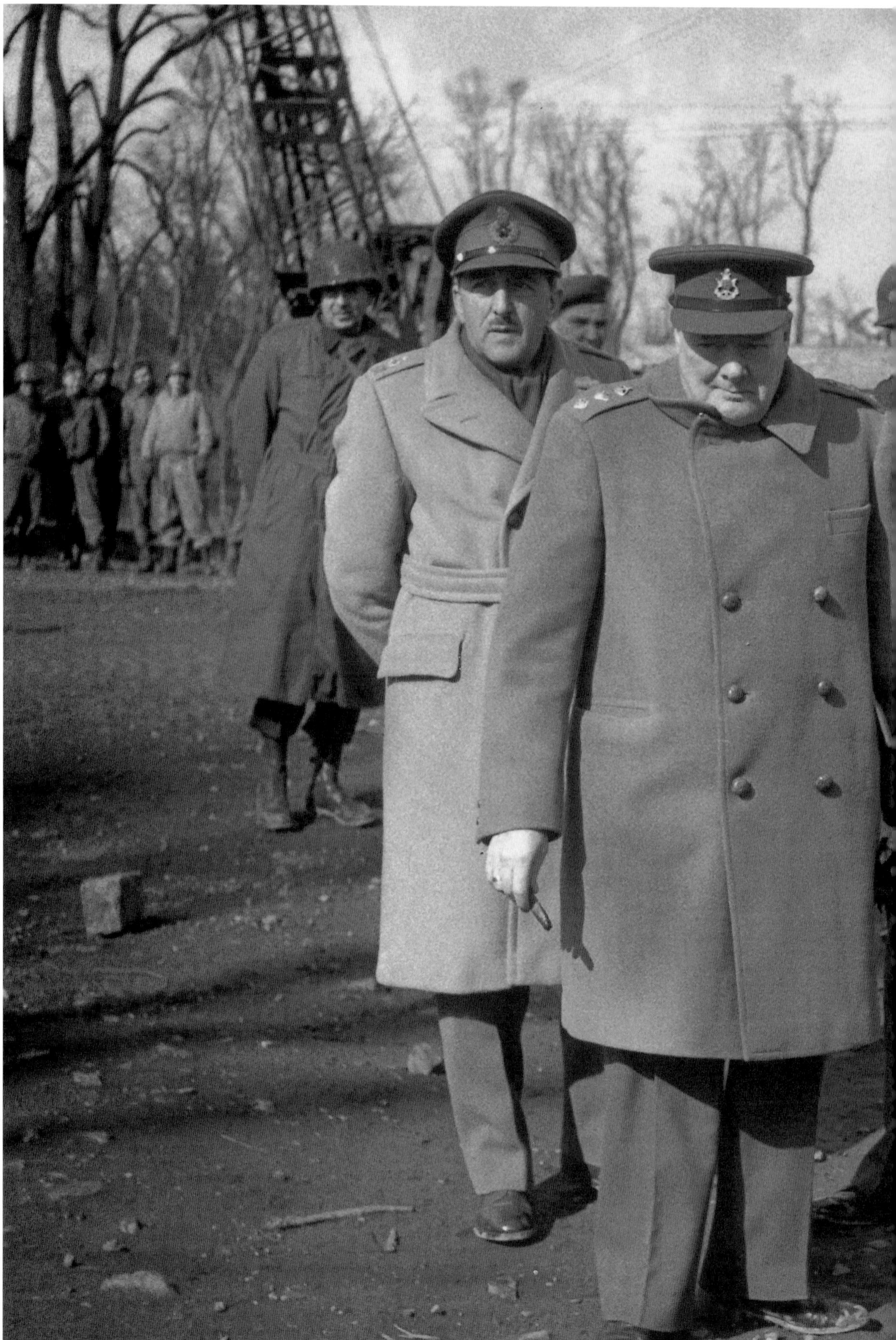

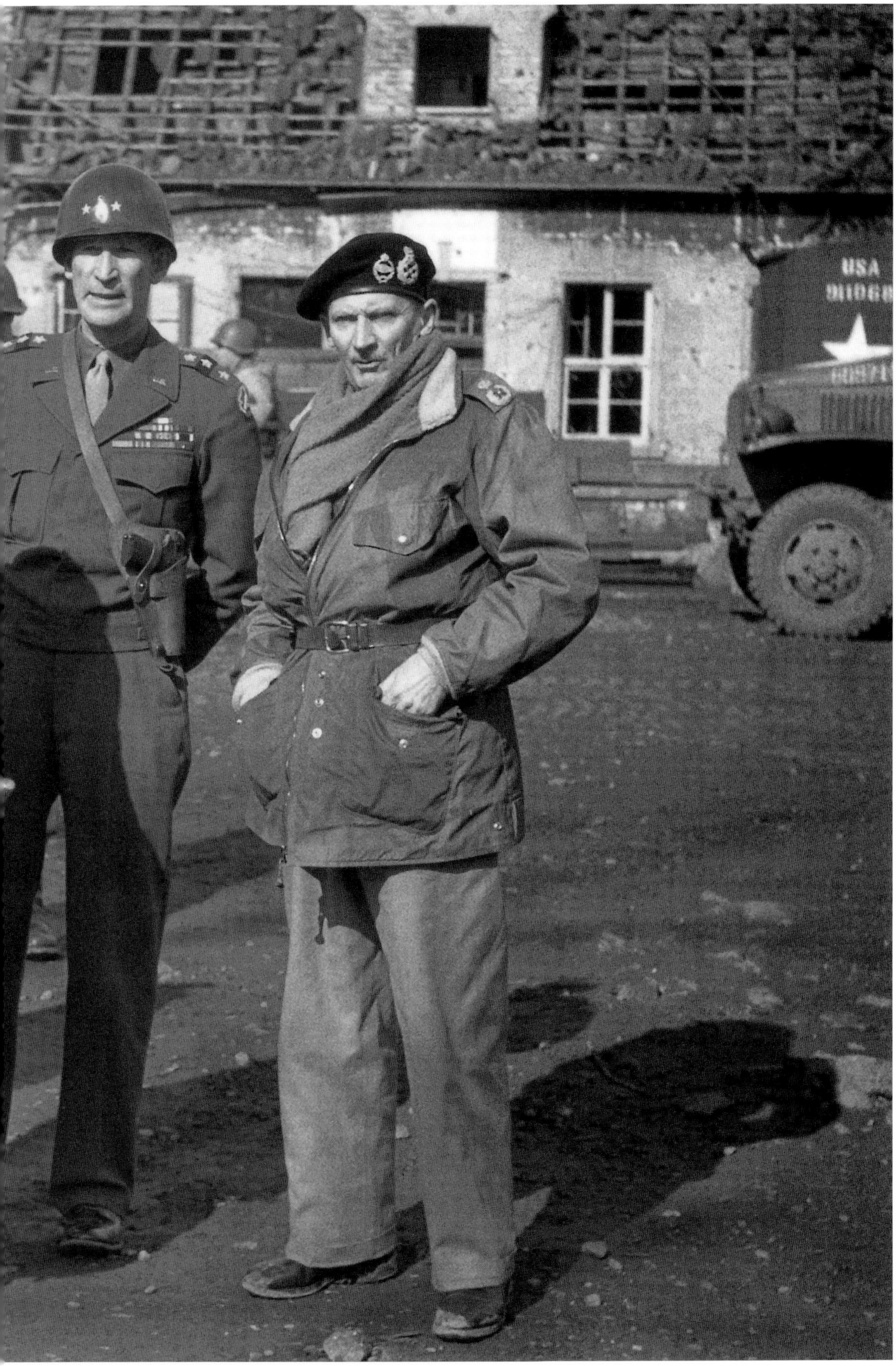
USA

reinforcements to the invasion area. He was, however, unsuccessful in convincing Eisenhower that the controversial Operation Anvil (later renamed Dragoon), the planned diversionary attack in southern France, would constitute an unnecessary waste of resources and this was merely postponed.

The final blueprint for Overlord, fully endorsed by Eisenhower, which Montgomery unveiled with much fanfare on 7 April 1944, envisaged three phases: the landing and linking up of the beach-heads; expansion of the bridgehead; then breakout. Once the landing had been achieved, the British Second Army, under the command of Lieutenant-General Miles Dempsey, was rapidly to expand the eastern end of the bridgehead to include the road, rail, river and canal centre of Caen, and then advance south to Falaise. This would anchor the Allied left flank and provide a shield for

Patton's US Third Army and Lieutenant-General Omar Bradley's US First Army, which were to cut off and clear the Cotentin peninsula and capture the key port of Cherbourg. Once this had been achieved and sufficient forces built up, the Allied armies would then attempt to breakout eastwards towards the River Seine, which Montgomery hoped would be reached by the beginning of September. In the process, a lodgement area would be formed in the open terrain between Caen and Falaise, from which the Allies, supported by fighter-bombers relocated from England, could launch their advance beyond the Seine.

Aided by a comprehensive deception plan, which sought to convince the Germans that the main assault would be launched against the Pas de Calais, and despite a 24 hour delay due to bad weather, D-Day was finally launched on 6 June 1944: the greatest amphibious operation ever mounted. It was preceded overnight by three separate airborne landings, by the US 82nd and 101st Airborne Divisions in the Carentan estuary and the British 6th Airborne Division north of Caen. Designed to take or destroy key strong points behind the invasion beaches, the most famous of these actions was the 6th Airborne's capture of the vital Pegasus Bridge that crossed the River Orne and the Orne canal between Caen and the sea. Also before dawn, more than 1,000 British aircraft saturated the German coastal defences with over 5,000 tons of bombs, a bombardment that was supplemented by the guns of the huge Allied invasion fleet. There were five invasion beaches in total. In the east, elements of the British Second Army successfully landed on Sword, Juno and Gold beaches in the Caen sector and within two and a half hours, 30,000 men, 300 guns and 700 armoured vehicles had made it ashore. To the west, in the American

D-DAY AND THE BATTLE OF NORMANDY

OVERLEAF: **Churchill and Montgomery ride along one of the Normandy invasion beaches, 12 June 1944. Churchill had crossed the Channel in the British destroyer HMS Kelvin and received a great welcome from troops unloading stores on the beach. He remained in France for seven hours, driving towards the battle zone and visiting Allied troops.**

BELOW: **The Normandy battlefield.**

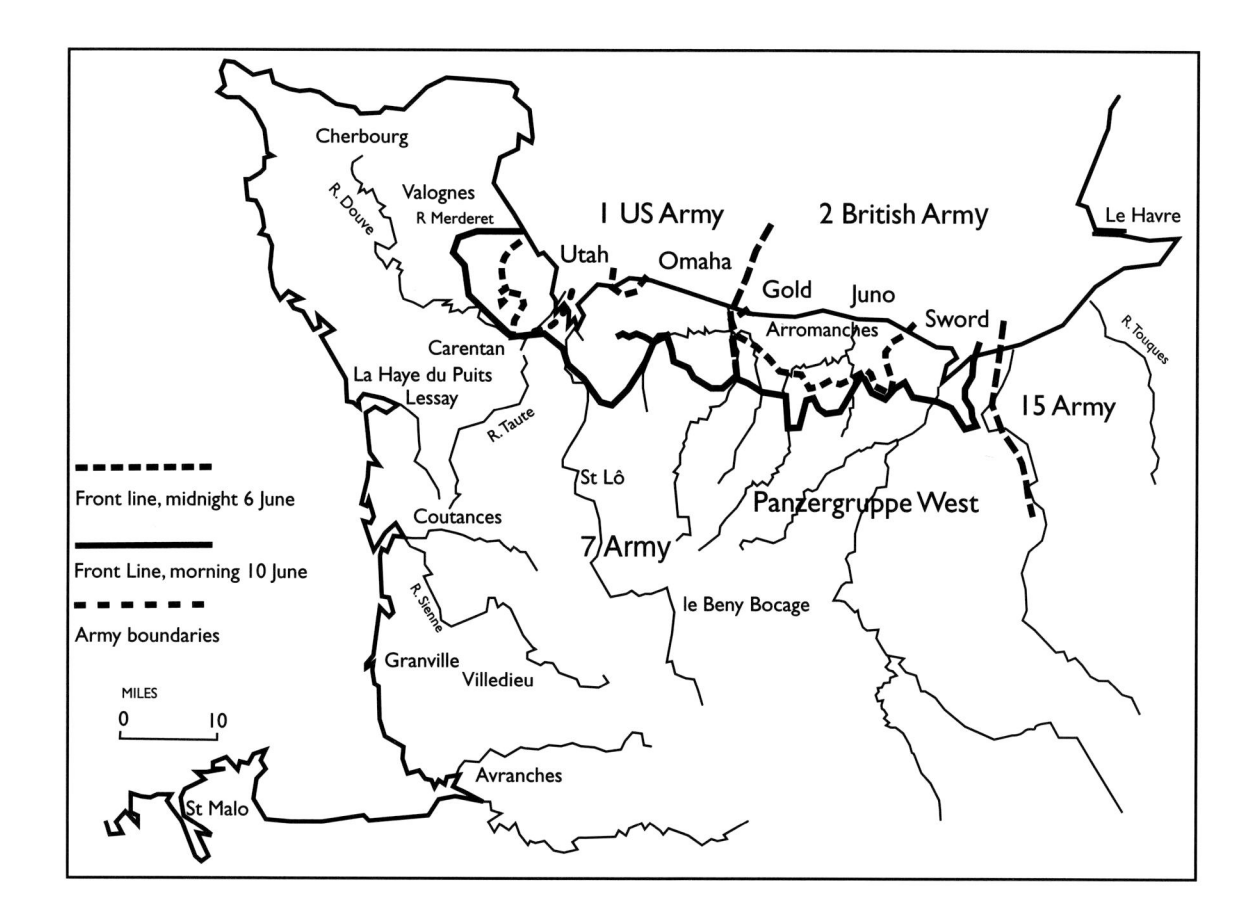

T69

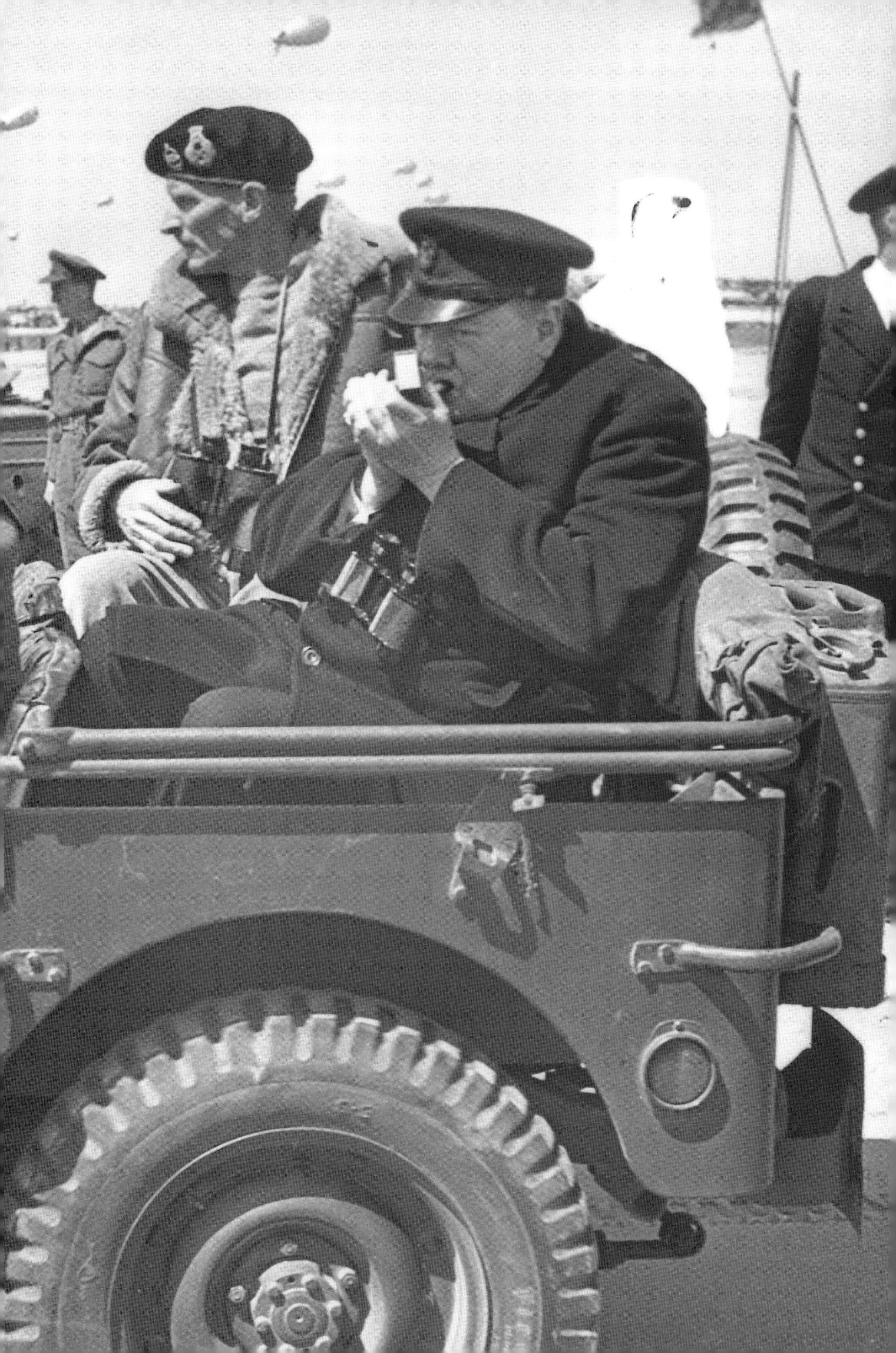

sector, the Utah beach assault achieved complete surprise and the opposition was so slight that very few casualties were sustained. The second American landing on Omaha beach however, met fierce resistance from the German 325th Division, which had escaped the attention of Allied intelligence. Throughout the day, the position on Omaha beach was extremely tenuous and evacuation was considered, but after many individual acts of bravery, the beachhead was finally secured. By the end of the day, despite the best efforts of the Germans, whose response had been compromised by the failure to commit their mobile reserves until it was too late, the Allies had succeeded in establishing a secure beachhead in Normandy.

OVERLEAF: **Lieutenant General George S. Patton, Commander of the US Third Army (left) and Lieutenant General Omar N. Bradley, Commander of the 12th US Army Group (middle), discuss the progress of the Normandy campaign with Montgomery.**

The overwhelming success of D-Day was a triumph for Montgomery. Although losses exceeded 10,000, a total of 155,000 troops had been landed, including 23,000 airborne troops. In an acknowledgement of this, Montgomery came ashore on 8 June, while the likes of Bradley remained at sea. He established his tactical headquarters a mere three miles from the front line. Nevertheless, Montgomery's master plan fell short in one key respect. Severe congestion in the beachheads had slowed the advance inland and many of the objectives which Montgomery had set for the end of D-Day had not been reached. The most notable of these was the city of Caen, central to Montgomery's overall strategy.

Much of the Normandy countryside was composed of *bocage* – small fields ringed by hedge-topped banks – and the German forces, under the overall command of Montgomery's old adversary Rommel,

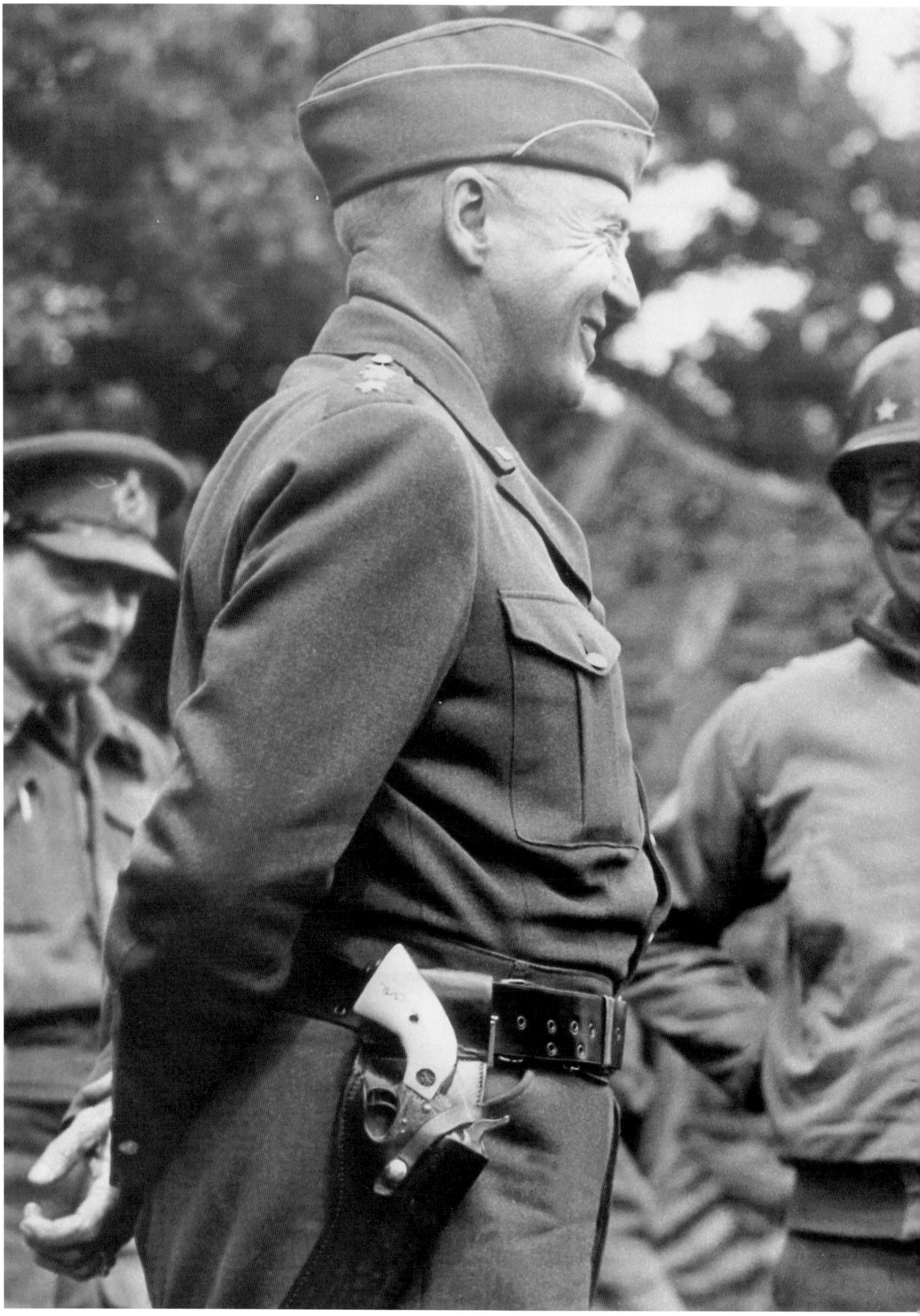

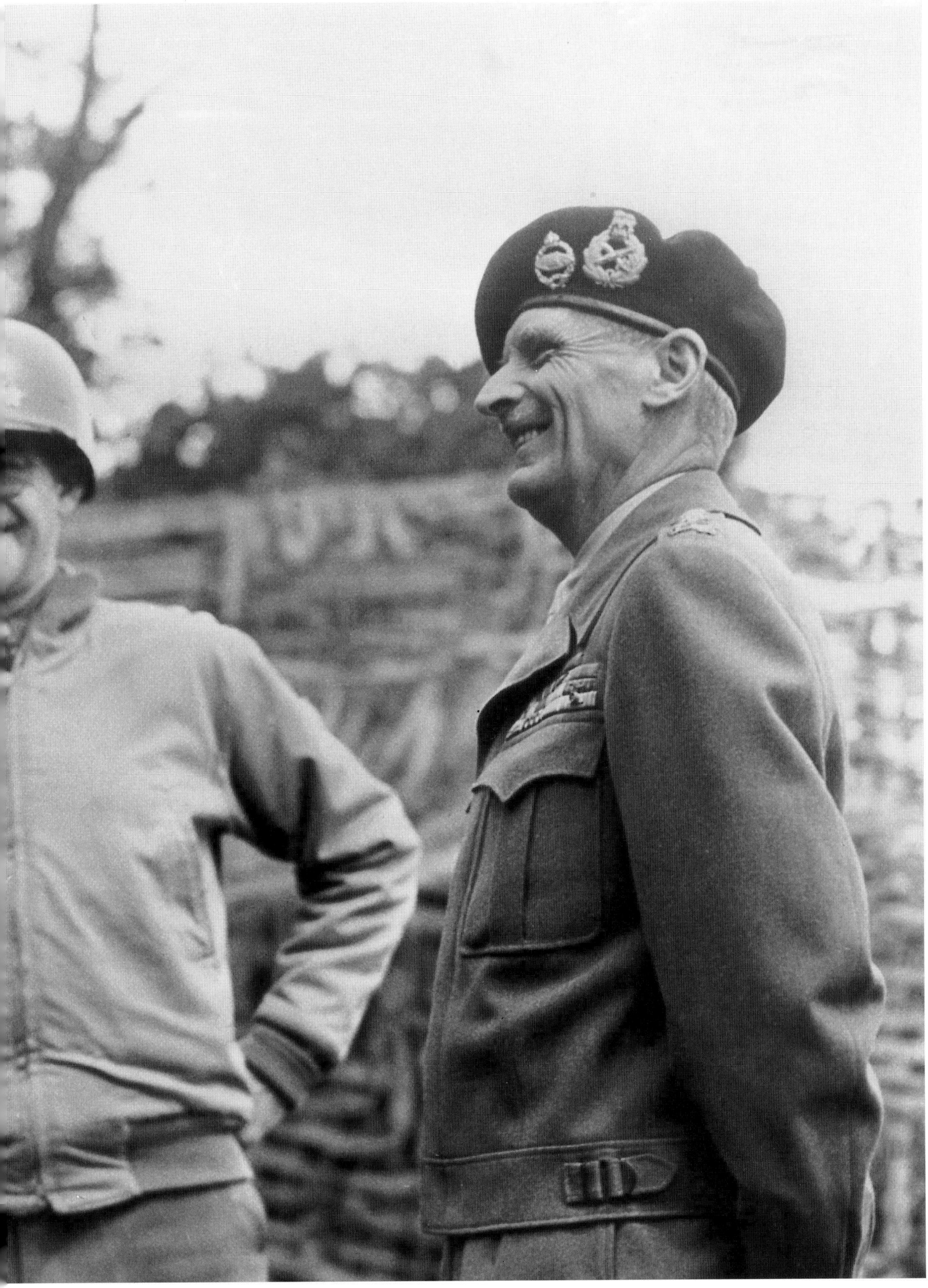

skilfully used the defensive qualities of the terrain to great advantage and exacted a heavy toll on the British forces, particularly their armour. By contrast, the performance of the British Second Army was often poor. Upon the insistence of Montgomery, three veteran divisions of Eighth Army composed the vanguard of Dempsey's army in order to provide a stabilizing influence. In the event, however, two of them, the 51st Highland Division and the famous 7th 'Desert Rats' Armoured Division, fought poorly and were overcautious in the *bocage*, while the 50th Northumbrian Division performed so badly that it was eventually disbanded. Casualties were high throughout the infantry. Officers were dying at a particularly high rate, causing the performance of junior officers to suffer as the more able were promoted to fill the gaps. As a result, morale suffered and was further diminished by the battles of attrition that now developed around Caen.

Once the British Second Army's initial thrust towards Caen had been halted, the Germans prepared a solid defence of the city, which was founded on dug-in tanks and anti-tank guns, most notably the PzKw VI 'Tiger' tank and the famous 88mm dual-purpose gun. The German defence was steadily reinforced as Rommel's armoured divisions slowly made their way towards Caen, despite the best efforts of Allied aircraft. Montgomery first attempted a pincer movement around Caen, supported by an airborne drop to the south of the city. However, the airborne drop was vetoed and, in the face of fierce resistance, neither of the ground thrusts made significant headway between 12-15 June. A second attempt, designed to envelop Caen from the west by launching a powerful thrust across the River Odon, was postponed following a severe storm in the Channel from 18 - 21 June, which seriously interfered with the build-up of supplies and reinforcements. The plan was subsequently resurrected as Operation Epsom and was entrusted to the newly arrived VIII Corps, commanded by Lieutenant-General Sir Richard O'Connor, a veteran of the North African campaign, who had escaped from an Italian prisoner of war camp the previous year. The resulting battle, which commenced on 26 June, quickly turned into one of the costliest of the war. O'Connor's attack was contested by no less than eight German armoured divisions, who had heavily fortified Hill 112, a formidable position that commanded the ground to the south of Caen. Unsurprisingly, VIII Corps' attack was soon halted on the southern side of the River Odon, where it was relentlessly counter-attacked by five of the German divisions during the first few days of July. O'Connor nevertheless held firm and inflicted heavy casualties on the Germans; in fact, losses on both sides were so high that the river became dammed up with corpses, causing it to be dubbed the 'Bloody Odon'.

Montgomery's next attempt coincided with a major offensive by Bradley's US First Army which, having secured the port of Cherbourg, attacked southwards between Caumont and St Lo on

OVERLEAF: **Montgomery opens the one thousandth Bailey Bridge built by British engineers since D-Day, 14 April 1945.**

3 July. Designed to bypass the *bocage* and swing south and south-east, Bradley's attack soon bogged down short of St Lo while to the east, Dempsey managed to secure the northern half of Caen in a direct assault. This fresh attack had been preceded by Operation Charnwood on 10 July, in which heavy bombers reduced much of the medieval city to ruins. Although this tactic certainly cowed the German defenders, at least for a while, the rubble and cratering caused by the bombing severely restricted the mobility of the attackers, especially that of the armour. Consequently, the city to the north of the River Orne was captured only after two days of bitter fighting, while efforts to evict the enemy south of the river whose bridges had been demolished, had petered out by mid-July.

By now, with both the British and American's progress checked, it appeared that Overlord might become stalemated in much the same

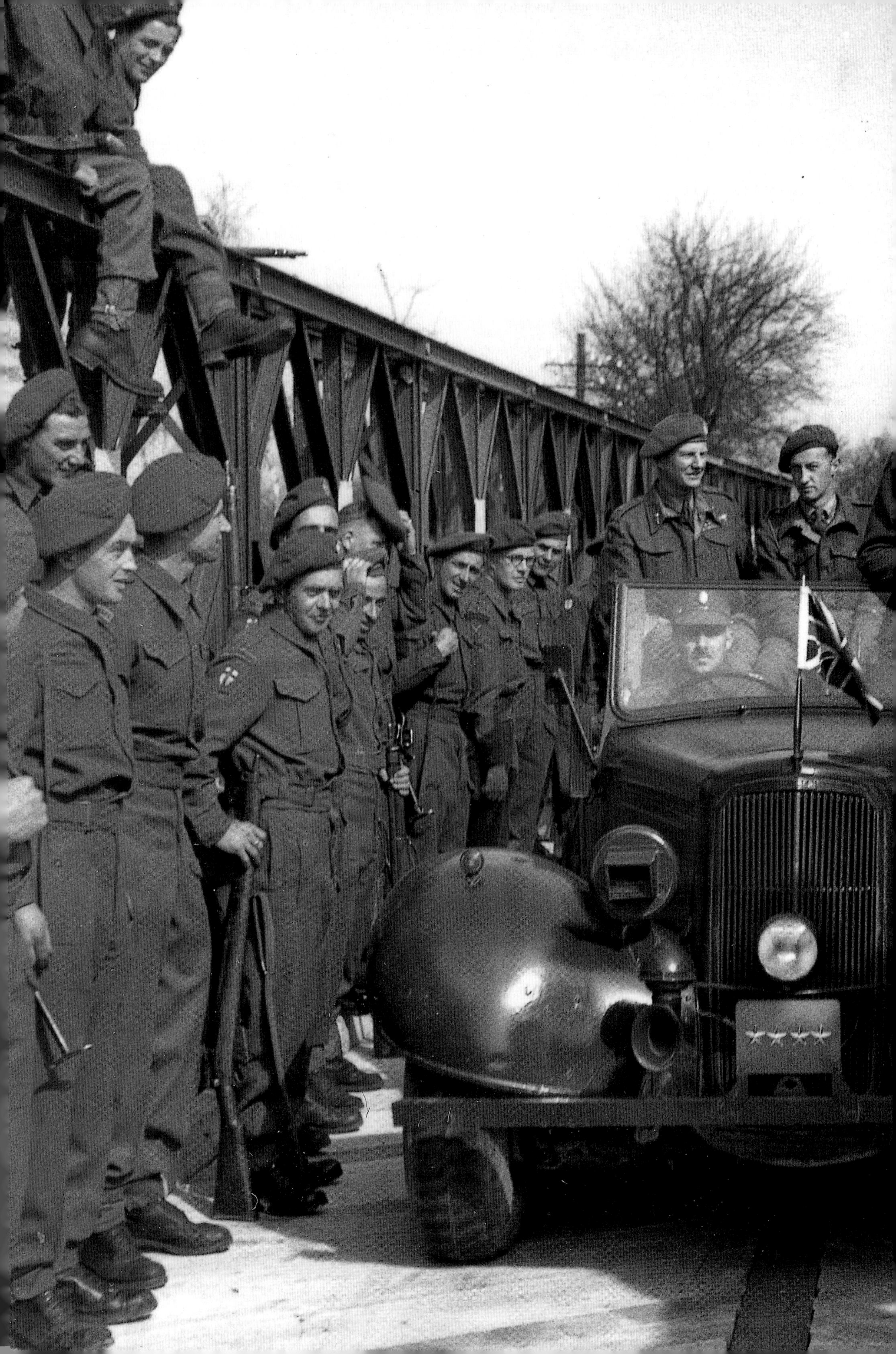

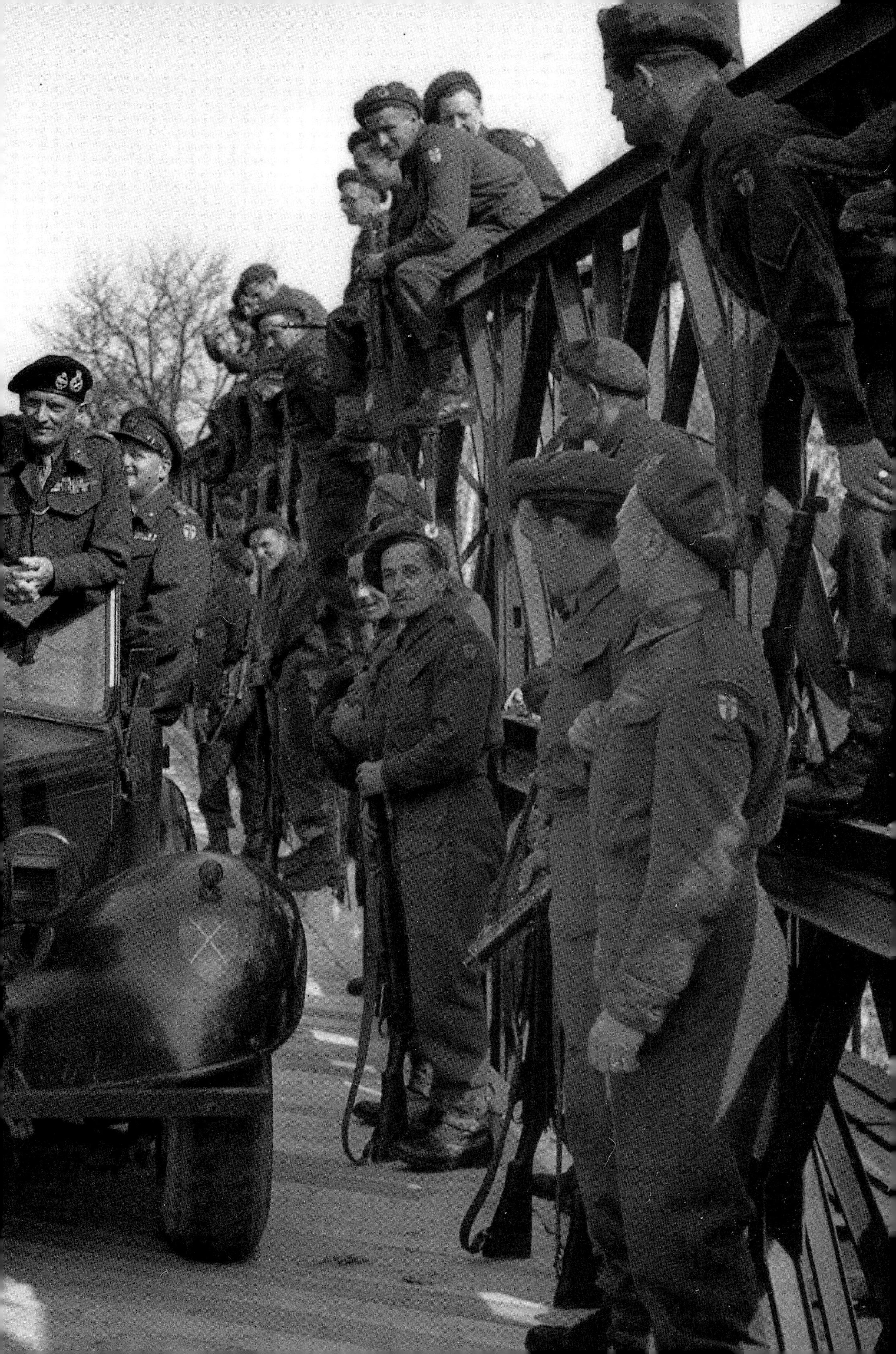

way as the Western Front had done in the First World War. Montgomery's failure to capture Caen was steadily eroding his reputation. His critics back home, most notably Eisenhower's staff and senior RAF officers who were eyeing up the open country south of Caen for the construction of airfields, were growing increasingly impatient. So much so that, egged on by the British and American press, both Eisenhower and Churchill were under extreme pressure to relieve him of his command. Moreover, increasing casualties among the British Second Army's infantry and the severe shortage of

RIGHT: **Montgomery with his two puppies named 'Hitler' and 'Rommel'.**

OVERLEAF: **Montgomery visits ex-prisoners-of-war at Stalag 118, near Falling Bostel, shortly before their journey home.**

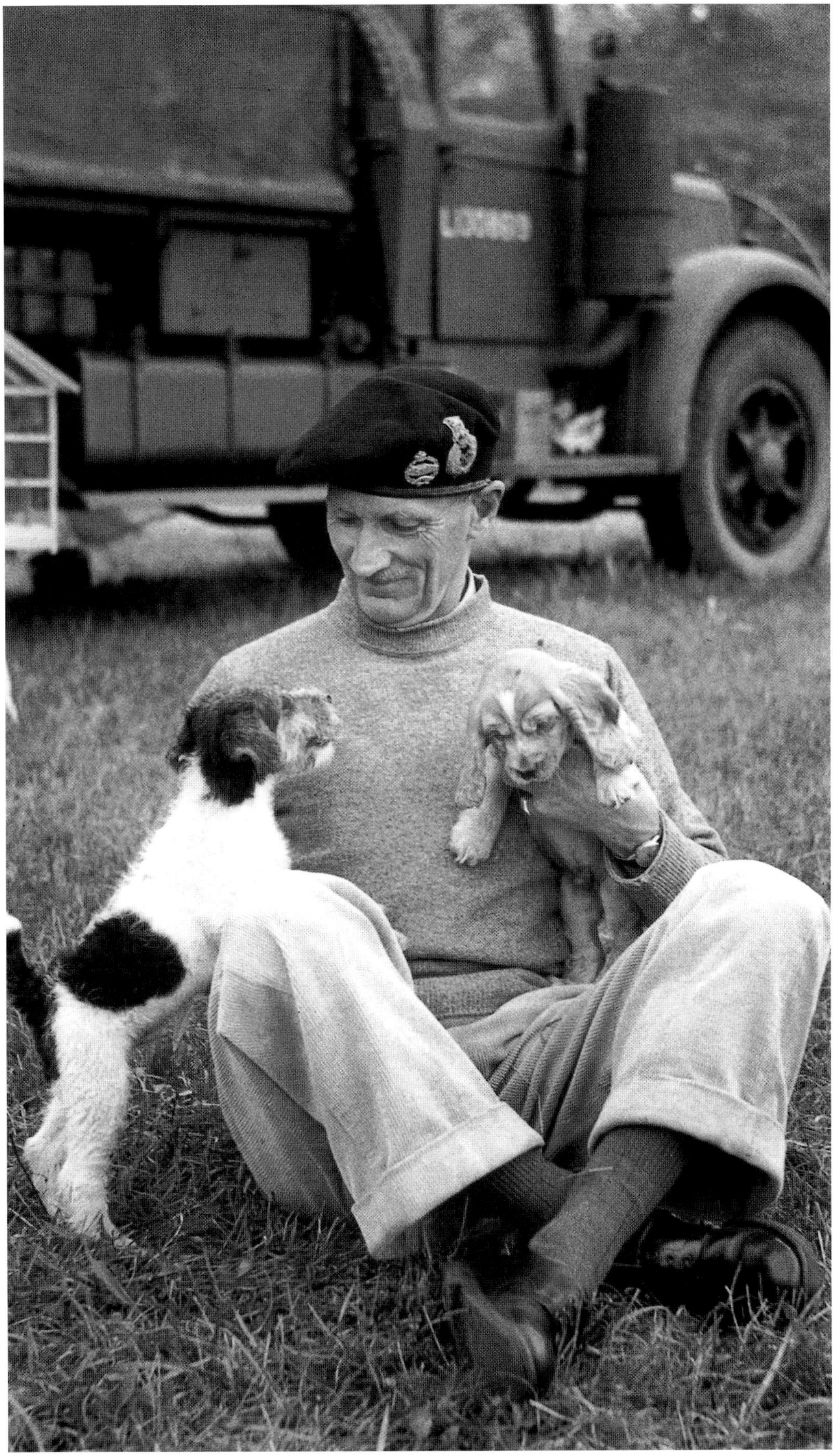

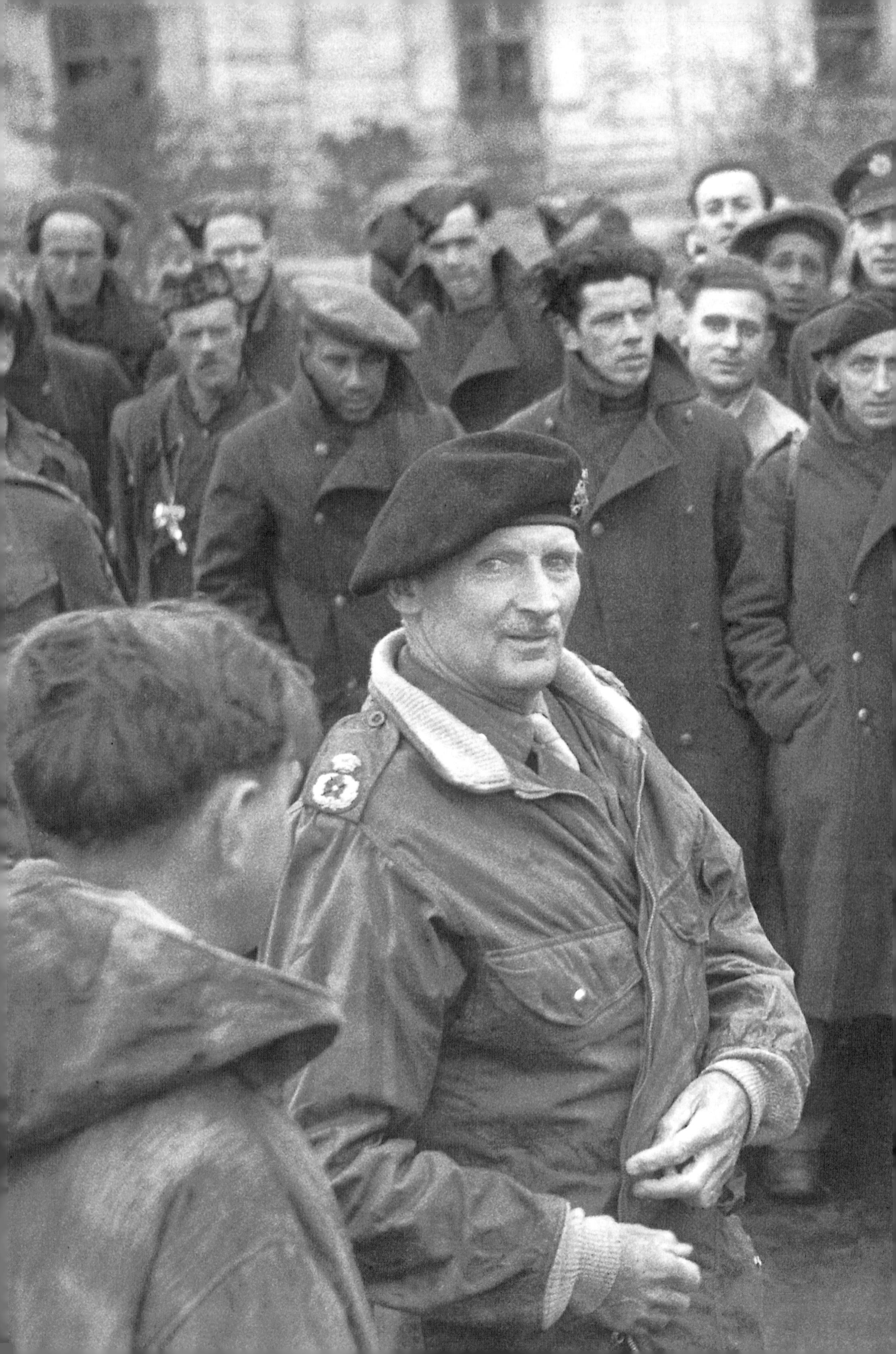

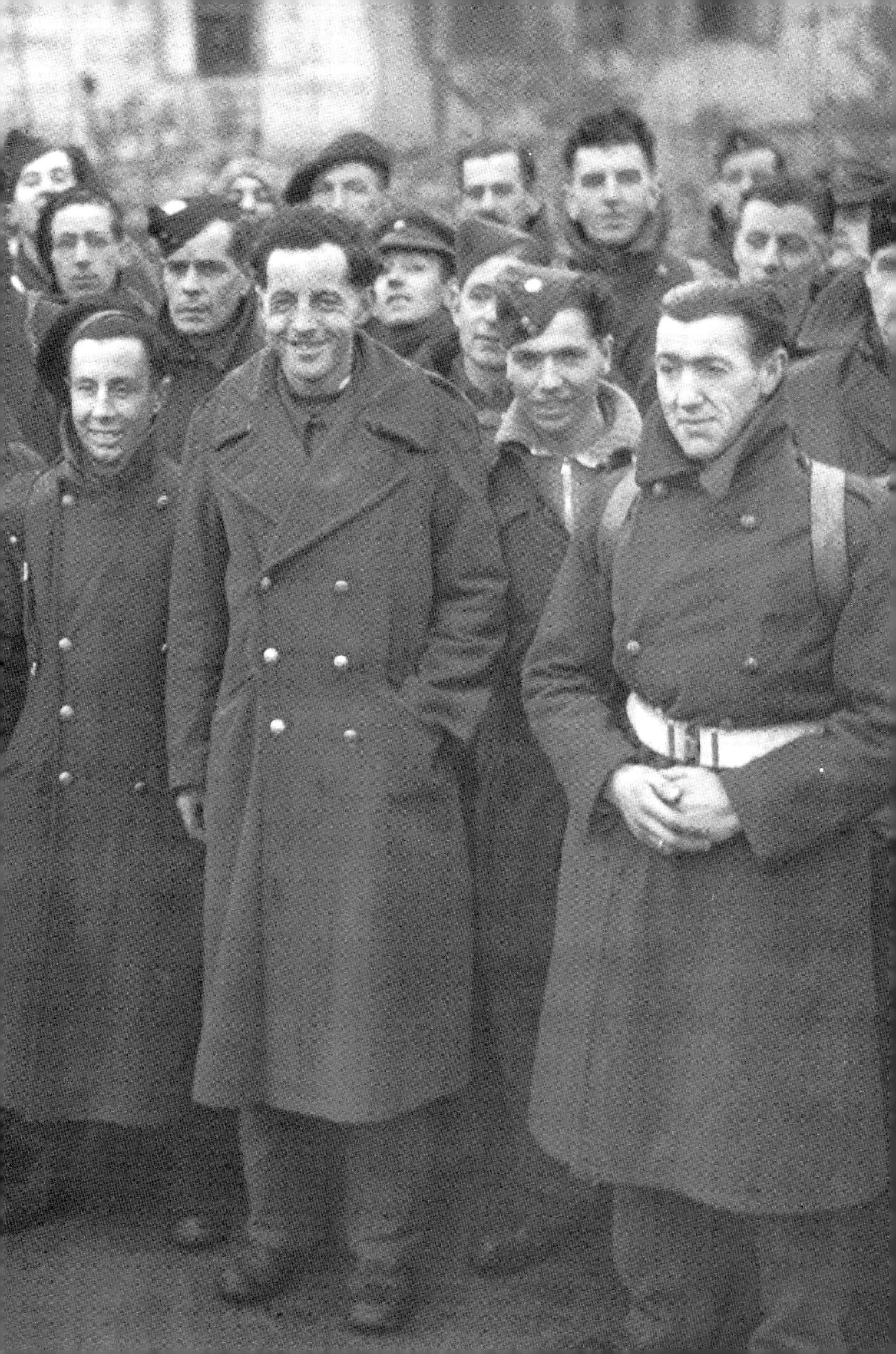

replacements were causing acute disillusionment, particularly concerning Montgomery's assertion that each new effort would lead to a breakthrough. Montgomery therefore decided to direct his next attack, Operation Goodwood, to the east of Caen, aiming at the open countryside of the Caen-Falaise plain, which on this occasion, would be predominantly an armoured attack. Preceded by a heavy bombardment by RAF bombers, three armoured divisions, flanked on the right by Canadian infantry and by British infantry on the left, launched the attack on 18 July. However, after two days of heavy fighting, Goodwood had managed only to clear the southern suburbs of Caen and penetrate a maximum of six miles into the countryside beyond.

This further failure to break the stalemate attracted still more criticism of Montgomery, who exacerbated his predicament by claiming a level of success for Goodwood that far exceeded the reality. It was at this point, however, that events began to turn in Montgomery's favour. Following an extremely costly battle, Bradley finally secured St Lo on 19 July and was able to prepare a breakout attempt, codenamed Operation Cobra, which was unleashed on 25 July. The offensive began with the increasingly popular tactic of a heavy bomber attack on the German positions, which on this occasion was concentrated on an area to the west of St Lo, measuring just 6,000 yards wide and 2,400 yards deep. Although the air bombardment caused 700 American casualties, its intensity aided the initial thrust by three infantry divisions of the American VII Corps, which gained a hard-fought mile on the first day. Two armoured divisions were released into the fray at first light on 26 July and, after six days, a definite breakout had been achieved. Responding quickly to this development, Montgomery switched the British Second Army's effort to the west of Caen to aid Bradley's push. Operation Bluecoat saw VIII Corps thrust south from Caumont towards Vire and, on their left, XXX Corps advanced towards Mont Pincon while the Canadian First Army took over to the east of Caen and continued the push towards Falaise. Meantime, the newly formed US Third Army, under the command of Patton, had broken out to the south into Brittany, through a narrow corridor near Avranches, on 1 August.

In response to Patton's breakout, Hitler ordered the German Seventh Army to launch a counter-attack westwards towards Mortain. This order soon proved fatal, however, as it exposed the German forces to possible entrapment in what became known as the Falaise pocket. While the US First and Third Armies exerted pressure from the south, VIII and XXX Corps steadily drove the Germans into the trap from the west. Meantime, Montgomery ordered the Canadian First Army to form the north side of the trap by advancing on Falaise. After fierce fighting, Falaise finally fell, but not until 16 August, by which time Patton had reached Argentan, 25 miles to the south. At this point, confusion reigned over exactly where the pocket should be closed. Bradley ordered Patton to cease his advance northwards as he feared his forces would become confused with the Canadians. In the event, the encirclement was not completed until 21 August, when the Canadian 2nd Corps, including the Polish 1st Armoured Division, had to fight off a desperate series of attacks by 1st SS Panzer Corps as the Germans struggled to keep their escape route open. Although some German elements did manage to escape from the Falaise pocket, those left behind were smashed by the Allied air forces. In all, the Falaise pocket claimed over 700 tanks and armoured fighting vehicles and almost 1,000 guns, while their dead numbered 10,000 and 50,000 more were captured. Some 20,000 troops, 24 tanks and 60 guns escaped to the east across the river Seine, but of the 50 German divisions present in Normandy in June, only ten remained that were worthy of the name.

The closing of the Falaise pocket effectively ended the Battle of Normandy. With the German forces in headlong retreat, the Allies established their first lodgement over the Seine on 19 August and Paris was liberated, without serious fighting, six days later. Although the campaign had not unfolded the way Montgomery had anticipated, the forces under his command had nevertheless reached the Seine earlier than envisaged in his original plan. In the process, a heavy defeat had been inflicted on the enemy. German casualties have been estimated at 450,000, including 210,000 prisoners-of-war. In addition, 1,500 tanks and 3,500 guns were lost. The Allied victory had nevertheless come at a price (209,672 casualties, of which 36,976 were killed), testament to the tenacious defence put up by the German Army. However, Hitler's insistence that the battle be fought well forward, with the intention of forcing the Allies back into the sea, had ultimately resulted in the mass carnage at Falaise. With the French capital liberated, the road to Germany was seemingly open and unguarded.

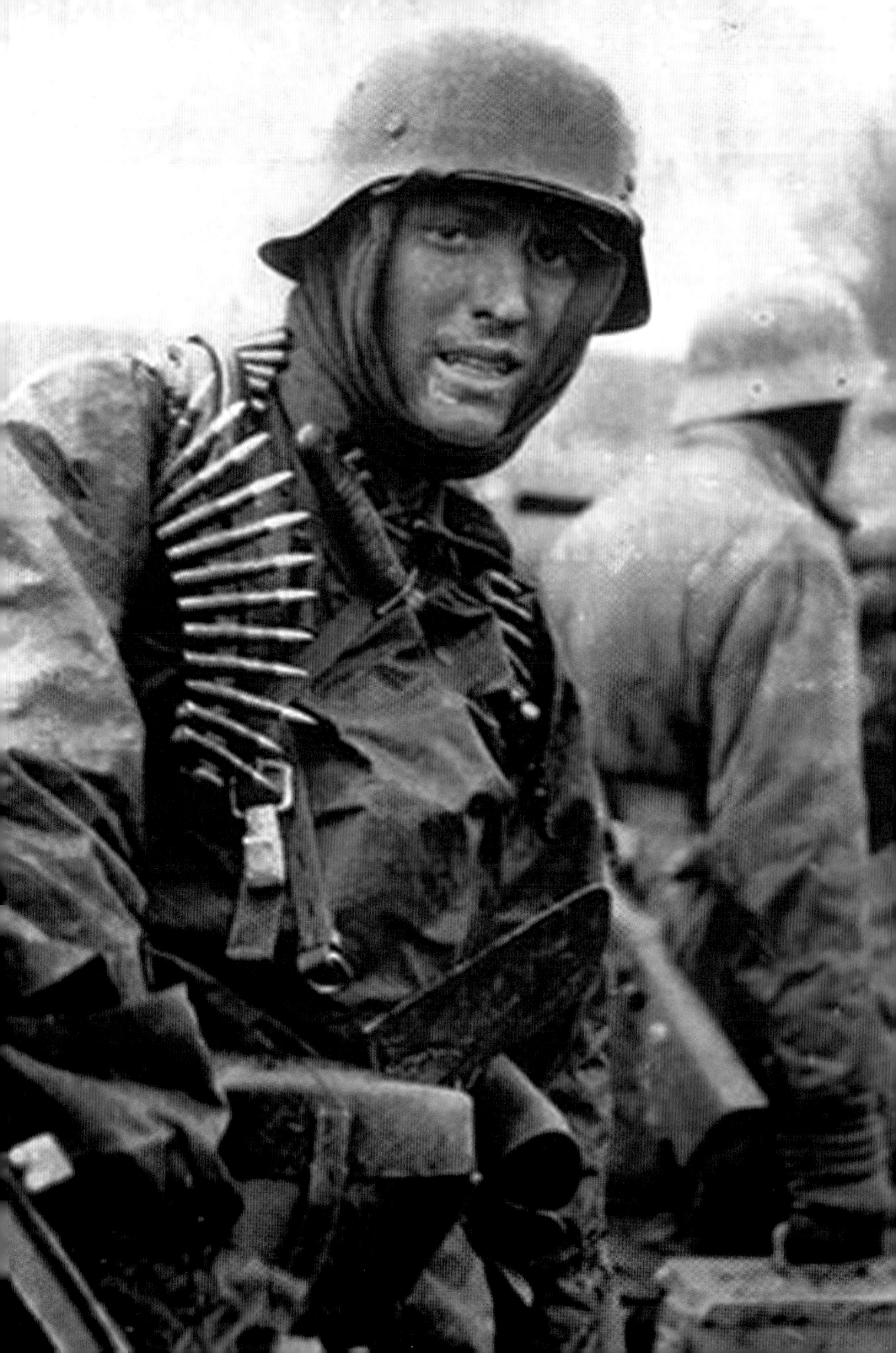

CHAPTER 5

FROM ARNHEM TO FINAL SURRENDER

THE ULTIMATE SUCCESS of Operation Overlord nevertheless left a bitter-sweet taste in Montgomery's mouth for, on 1 September, as had been agreed beforehand, he relinquished overall command of the Allied forces to Eisenhower. At the same time, his 21st Army Group was reduced in size to just the Canadian First and British

LEFT: **A heavily armed German soldier carrying ammunition boxes during the Battle of the Bulge, December 1944.**

Second Armies and now operated alongside the Twelfth US Army Group, commanded by the newly promoted Bradley, which included the US First Army and Patton's US Third Army. Although these changes coincided with Montgomery's promotion to Field-Marshal, he had, in effect, been demoted to a position equal to that of his former subordinate Bradley. Moreover, although British and Canadian forces had been in the majority during the D-Day landings, from that point on the American preponderance in men and material became increasingly marked. These factors created the foundation for the serious tensions that were soon to erupt between Montgomery and Eisenhower, particularly over the latter's future prosecution of the campaign.

With the German forces in full-scale withdrawal, Eisenhower's first major decision was to scrap the pre-planned halt and regrouping on the Seine in favour of an immediate pursuit. Intended to finish off the German army before it could mount an effective defence of the Third Reich's borders, Eisenhower's broad front strategy reflected the general euphoria that now swept through the Allied armies. Believing that the Germans were close to collapse and that one last major effort would end the war that autumn, Eisenhower issued a directive on 4 September, that called for a broad advance by all the Allied armies to the German frontier, whereupon they would await a suitable opportunity to strike into Germany itself. In accordance with what Eisenhower described as 'bulling ahead on all fronts', Montgomery's 21st Army Group was ordered to advance through Belgium towards the Ruhr, the industrial heartland of Germany, while Twelfth Army Group would head towards the Saarland to the south, thus covering Montgomery's right flank. Indeed, the highly fluid nature of the campaign in late-August and early September appeared to vindicate Eisenhower's strategy. While the US Seventh and French First Armies, landed in the south of France on 15 August during Operation Dragoon, moved rapidly northwards, both Bradley and Montgomery were advancing at a stunning rate. Under the command of the latter, the Canadian First Army began to clear the heavy German presence in the Pas de Calais and the Scheldt estuary around Antwerp, while the spearhead of the British Second Army, XXX Corps, smashed their way across the French border into southern Belgium at the rate of 50 miles a day. Brussels was liberated by the British on 3 September and Antwerp was reached the following day. However, at this point, an uncharacteristically bold Montgomery committed a significant strategic error. Instead of completely clearing the Scheldt estuary and thereby opening the vital port of Antwerp, he entertained the ambitious plan of encircling the Ruhr via rapid thrusts across the Meuse and Rhine rivers.

Montgomery's decision was politically motivated. Aware of the growing preponderance of American forces within the alliance, Montgomery hoped that British forces could secure victory in the west before the United States became totally dominant.

Montgomery's failure to quickly open up the port of Antwerp effectively ended any hopes that the Allies had of bringing the war to a swift conclusion. The sheer pace of the Allied advance had created huge logistical problems. Because of Hitler's order to defend to the last the Channel and the French Atlantic ports, the Allied armies were still being supplied from Cherbourg, some 300 miles to the rear. Therefore, despite American efforts to move supplies by the means of a conveyor belt of trucks, known as the Red Ball Express, severe fuel shortages caused the Allied pursuit to peter out in the second week of September. These logistical problems were compounded by stiffening

German resistance. Between 19 and 31 August, the Germans had managed to safely ferry 240,000 men across the Seine and as the Allied advance ground to a halt, these troops began to form a new defence line stretching from the Channel to Switzerland, known by the defenders as the 'Miracle in the West'. Indeed, there was no Allied contingency plan in existence in the event that the Germans failed to collapse.

It was against these circumstances that Montgomery initiated a controversy that was to dog Allied relations until the end of the war.

RIGHT: **The devastated city of Nijmegen, Holland, with the Nijmegen Bridge over the River Waal in the background, 28 September 1944.**

FROM ARNHEM TO FINAL SURRENDER

From as early as mid-August, Montgomery began openly to criticize Eisenhower's broad front strategy, arguing that it was an unnecessary dispersal of effort that could not be maintained in view of the Allies' logistical problems. Instead, Montgomery repeatedly haranged Eisenhower with his own strategy, that of a narrow single thrust towards the northern Ruhr and thence on to Berlin. However, as we have seen, Eisenhower vetoed Montgomery's demands in his directive of 4 September, but the latter resurrected his plan upon reaching Antwerp. He demanded that 21st Army Group be given logistical priority and that a force of forty divisions under one commander, preferably himself, would be needed to execute the thrust. Under such pressure, Eisenhower compromised by affording Montgomery priority until he was beyond Antwerp, although he too failed to immediately emphasize the importance of clearing the Scheldt estuary before any further advance was attempted. Buoyed by this partial endorsement of his strategy, Montgomery intended to use the 1st Airborne Corps, under the command of Lieutenant-General F M Browning, to ease his crossing of the Meuse and the Rhine by seizing the bridges at Venlo and Wesel. However, Browning believed that such an action would be too much at risk from anti-aircraft fire and instead suggested to Montgomery that the whole First Allied Airborne Army, which had taken part in Overlord but had since lain idle, be used to turn the German flank by forcing a passage across the Lower Rhine in Holland. Browning's proposal fitted Montgomery's single-thrust strategy perfectly and with the Allied forces by now grinding to a halt, Montgomery was finally able to convince Eisenhower who, on 10 September, endorsed what became known as Operation Market Garden and promised 21st Army Group priority of supplies.

Under Montgomery's overall command, Browning assumed tactical control of Operation Market Garden which was composed of two parts. 'Market' involved the insertion of Lieutenant-General Lewis Brereton's First Allied Airborne Army behind enemy lines in Holland to capture and hold a number of vital bridges: over the canals at Eindhoven; the River Maas at Grave; the River Waal at Nijmegen and finally the Rhine at Arnhem. Eindhoven was entrusted to the US 101st Airborne Division, while their compatriots, the US 82nd Airborne Division, were assigned the bridges at Grave and Nijmegen. Meanwhile, the key bridges at Arnhem were the responsibility of the British 1st Airborne Division and the attached Polish 1st Independent Parachute Brigade. While this was taking place, the second phase of the operation, 'Garden', would see the British XXX Corps advance along the corridor opened up by the airborne troops and link up with each one in turn. Once in full control of the Arnhem bridge, the

British Second Army would then turn the German flank and assault the Ruhr through Germany's 'back-door', thus facilitating the collapse of the Third Reich by the end of the year. At the very least, Montgomery expected Market Garden to force the Germans out of Holland and therefore clear the Scheldt estuary.

On 17 September, after just seven days of planning, Operation Market Garden, the largest airborne assault in the history of warfare, was launched. Over 5,000 aircraft were involved and a total of 16,500 paratroopers and 3,500 troops in gliders were successfully and accurately landed and the two US airborne divisions managed to seize their objectives, while XXX Corps reached Eindhoven without major incident. Thereafter, however, the tactical shortcomings of the Market Garden plan quickly became apparent. Firstly, the British 1st Airborne Division was dropped some six miles from their objective and, secondly, because of the loss of their armoured jeep transport, it took elements of the division four hours to reach the bridges on foot, by which time the railway bridge had been destroyed. Although the northern end of the road bridge was eventually secured, the time taken had allowed German resistance to stiffen and much of the division was pinned down in and around Arnhem. The German

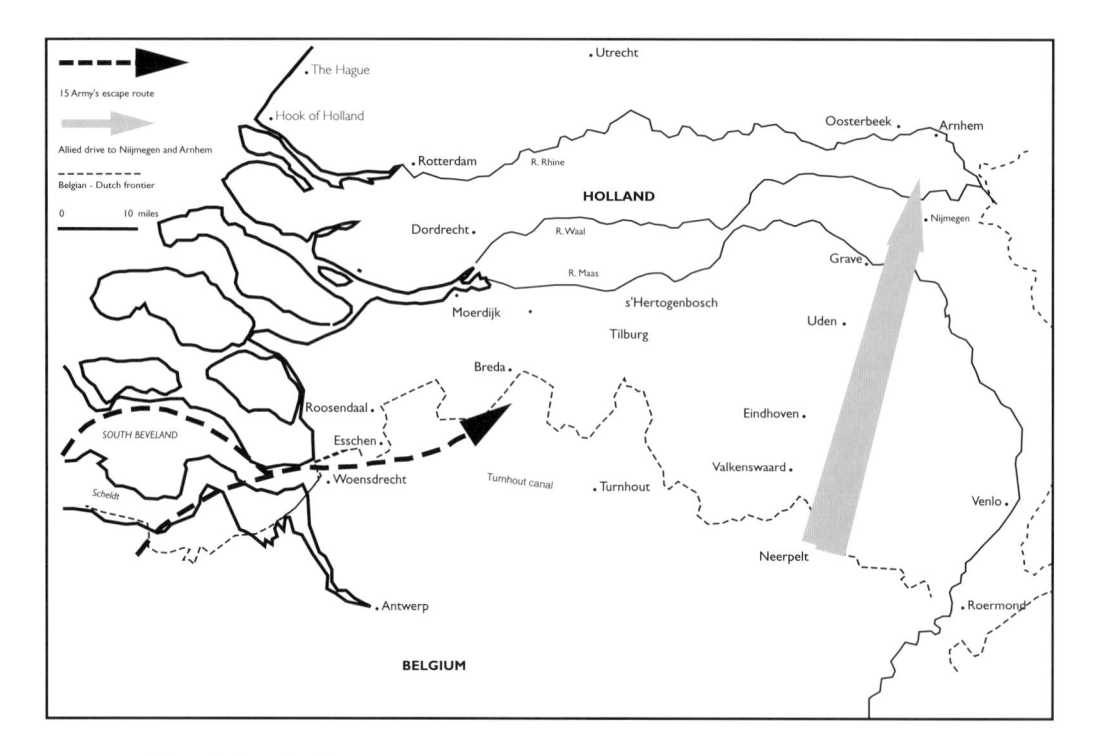

ABOVE: **The Scheldt Estuary and the route of Operation Market Garden.**

opposition centred on the remains of the 9th and 10th SS Panzer Divisions, which had been refitting outside the town and were fresh from an exercise in which they had practised how to defeat an airborne assault. The presence of these divisions had been known to Montgomery during the planning stage, but its significance had been either overlooked or ignored. The plight of the British paratroopers became even more acute when bad weather delayed their reinforcement by the Polish 1st Independent Parachute Brigade, and those that were landed were prevented from linking up with the British.

The key to the success of the whole operation, however, was the speed with which XXX Corps could link up and relieve the airborne troops. The plan required it to cover the 59 miles to Arnhem in three days, but by the time it reached Eindhoven it was already behind schedule. North of Eindhoven, XXX Corps found its progress further slowed by its confinement to a single narrow road because of the presence of wet lowlands on either side. This created considerable congestion and aided German attacks on its flanks. Meanwhile, the advance of the British VIII and XII Corps on either side of XXX Corps' corridor was, by Montgomery's own admission, 'depressingly slow'. Consequently, the bridges at Nijmegen were not secured until 20 September and XXX Corps did not begin its advance on Arnhem until the following day. By then, however, the 1st Airborne Division's position had become untenable and, although the leading elements had held on to the northern end of the bridge for four days, they were ultimately overrun. On 25 September, a decision to evacuate the remnants of the division was taken and some 2,400 British and Polish paratroopers were successfully withdrawn across the Rhine overnight. However, the division left behind 1,300 dead and 6,400 prisoners and was not reformed after the battle.

Montgomery commended the bravery of 1st Airborne Division, saying: 'In years to come it will be a great thing for a man to be able to say: "I fought at Arnhem".' These fine words failed to disguise the fact that Montgomery's ambitious plan had resulted in an ignominious defeat. In what has become popularly known as 'a bridge too far', Operation Market Garden failed to secure a bridgehead across the Rhine and ended any hopes of finishing the war by Christmas. Moreover, Montgomery now engaged in a fierce row with Eisenhower over his continuing failure to clear the Scheldt estuary. The failure of Market Garden to open up either Rotterdam or Amsterdam as alternative supply ports to Antwerp did not galvanize Montgomery into making the opening of Antwerp a top priority. Instead, he ignored intelligence that the Germans intended to make a stand on the Scheldt and gave the British Second Army's eastward advance favour over the Canadian First Army's approach to the river. Deprived of the necessary supplies, the Canadians were unable to prevent the evacuation of the whole German Fifteenth Army across the Scheldt into Holland. Under increasing pressure from Eisenhower, in mid-October Montgomery finally issued the Canadians with a clear directive to clear both banks of the Scheldt. A major attack was then launched which culminated, on 1 November, with an amphibious assault on the island of Walcheren, which guarded the mouth of the Scheldt estuary and had been heavily fortified by the Germans. After a week of often fierce fighting in appalling weather, the island was secured and Antwerp itself was declared open to shipping on 28 November, an event which significantly improved the Allies' supply situation.

For the remainder of the year, Montgomery employed his 21st Army Group in often attritional operations to clear Holland and Belgium up to and beyond the River Meuse, battles which secured little ground at high cost. While operations in Montgomery's sector degenerated into a weary stalemate, to the south, the Americans were suddenly hit by an audacious German counter-offensive on 16 December. In what subsequently became known as the 'Battle of the Bulge', Hitler's intention was to split the Allied armies and recapture Antwerp by means of a surprise thrust through the Ardennes region. Although the Germans caught the American defenders completely off-guard and made good early progress, by the end of the month their attack had been contained and clear skies, which had been absent at the start of the offensive, saw their forces subjected to heavy air attack.

OVERLEAF: **Montgomery addressing men of the British 1st Airborne Division.**

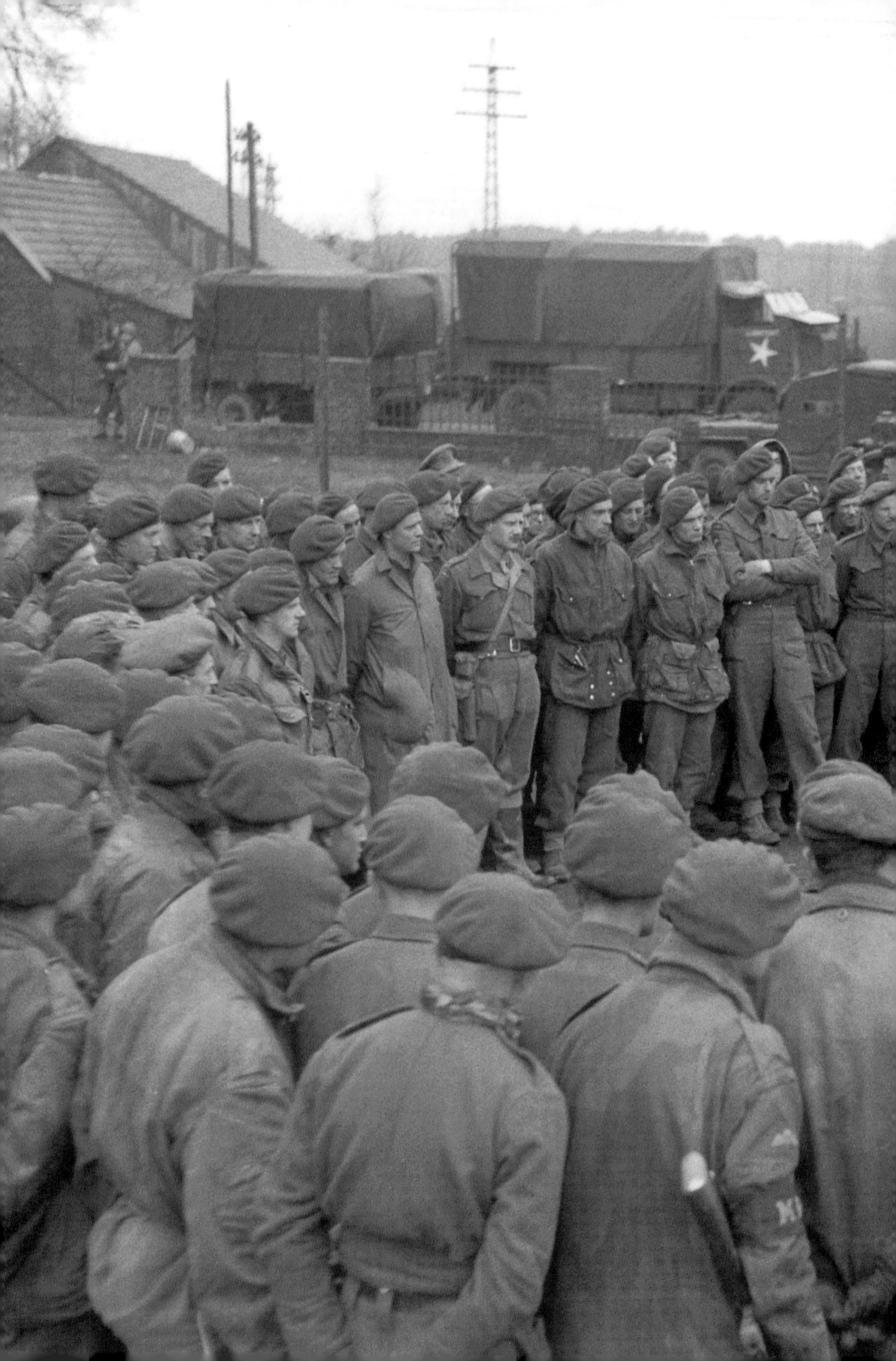

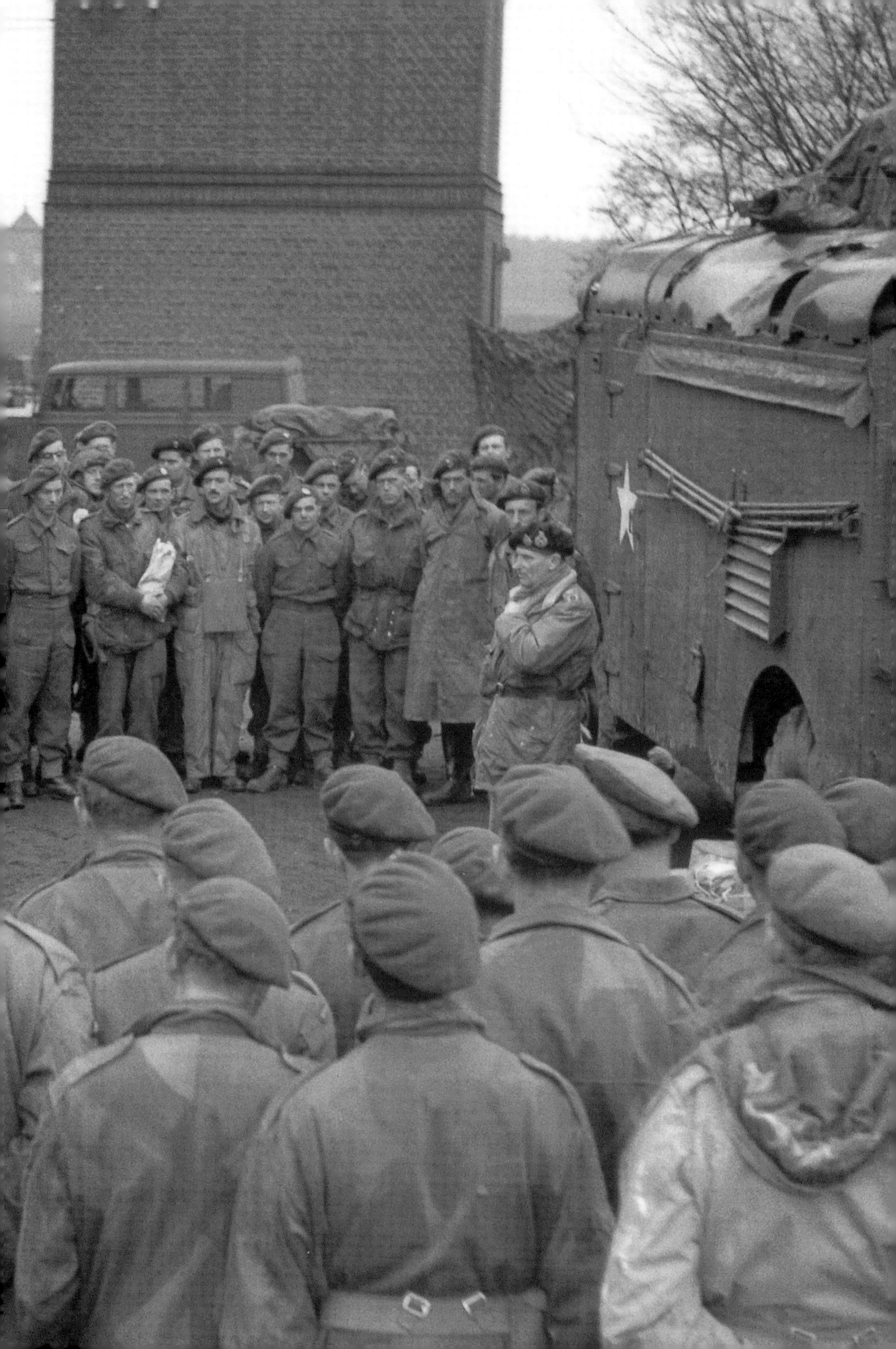

Montgomery's role in the battle was minimal. On 19 December, at the height of American panic and dislocation, Eisenhower reluctantly assigned command of Bradley's two northern armies to Montgomery, who then positioned elements of XXX Corps to head off any attempt by the Germans to cross the Meuse and capture Antwerp. In the event, XXX Corps saw very little action, but Montgomery's dispositions did help to stabilize the situation and enable the American armies further south to counter-attack.

Nevertheless, victory in the Battle of the Bulge was almost entirely an American feat-of-arms, achieved at the cost of 80,000 casualties. This did not, however, prevent Montgomery from damaging Allied relations still further when, on 7 January 1945, he held a press conference in which he paid tribute to Eisenhower and the American troops but also made thinly veiled suggestions that their initial reverses were of their own making. Describing the campaign as 'a most interesting little battle', Montgomery's ill-judged press conference brought the Allied high command structure close to breaking point. On the one hand, Bradley never forgave Montgomery for his comments while Eisenhower later claimed that the episode had caused him much distress. From that point on, Eisenhower, in the knowledge that American troops now outnumbered their British counterparts in the region of three-to-one, paid mere lip-service to Montgomery's strategic arguments when the whole broad-front versus narrow-front controversy was re-ignited in mid-January 1945, and the final offensives into Germany would be conducted on largely separate lines.

By 28 January, the Allies had reclaimed the ground lost during the German counter-offensive and on 1 February, it was Eisenhower's broad-fronted plan that was endorsed by the Combined Chiefs of Staff. In the north, Montgomery's 21st Army Group, comprising the British Second, Canadian First and the newly assigned US Ninth Army, would drive up to and across the Rhine north of the Ruhr and then advance over the North German plain in the direction of Berlin. Despite their soured relationship, Eisenhower accorded priority to Montgomery's offensive and the remaining French and three American armies, organized into the 12th US Army Group under Bradley and the 6th US Army Group under General Jacob Devers, would execute a strong secondary thrust south of the Ruhr only insofar as it did not denude Montgomery's effort. In all, almost four million British, American and Canadian troops now sat ready to launch the final battle.

Montgomery commenced his attack on 8 February, when the Canadian First Army, with XXX Corps attached, launched Operation

Veritable from the salient created by Market Garden. Intended to clear the Germans from the east of Nijmegen up to the Lower Rhine in preparation for the crossing of the river, Veritable opened with an artillery barrage from 1,050 guns, which enabled four divisions to break through part of the German's Siegfried Line on the second day. The Rhine was reached at Emmerich on 13 February but, thereafter, wintry conditions and determined resistance from the German First Parachute Army made the clearance of the Reichswald forest to the south a protracted and bitter struggle for the British and Canadian troops. It was not until the US Ninth Army began the delayed Operation Grenade on 23 February in support of Veritable, that significant progress was made. The American attack caught the distracted Germans off-balance and by 9 March, the two attacks had made contact and all remaining German forces had withdrawn across the Rhine. Veritable and Grenade had nevertheless cost Montgomery 23,000

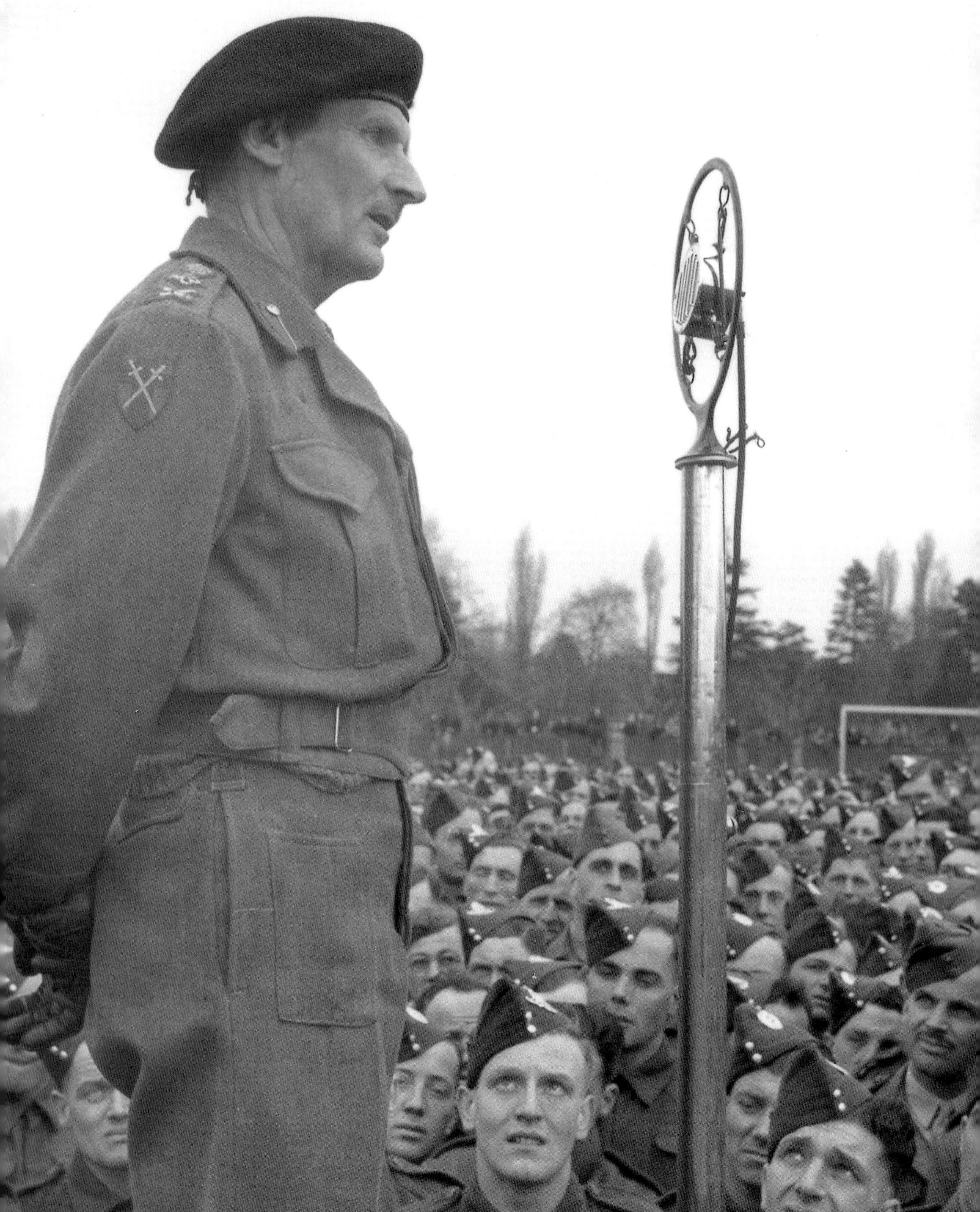

LEFT: **Montgomery regularly toured the theatre to speak to the troops he led during the liberation of Europe, travelling approximately 3,000 miles. Here, he addresses troops from the bonnet of a jeep.**

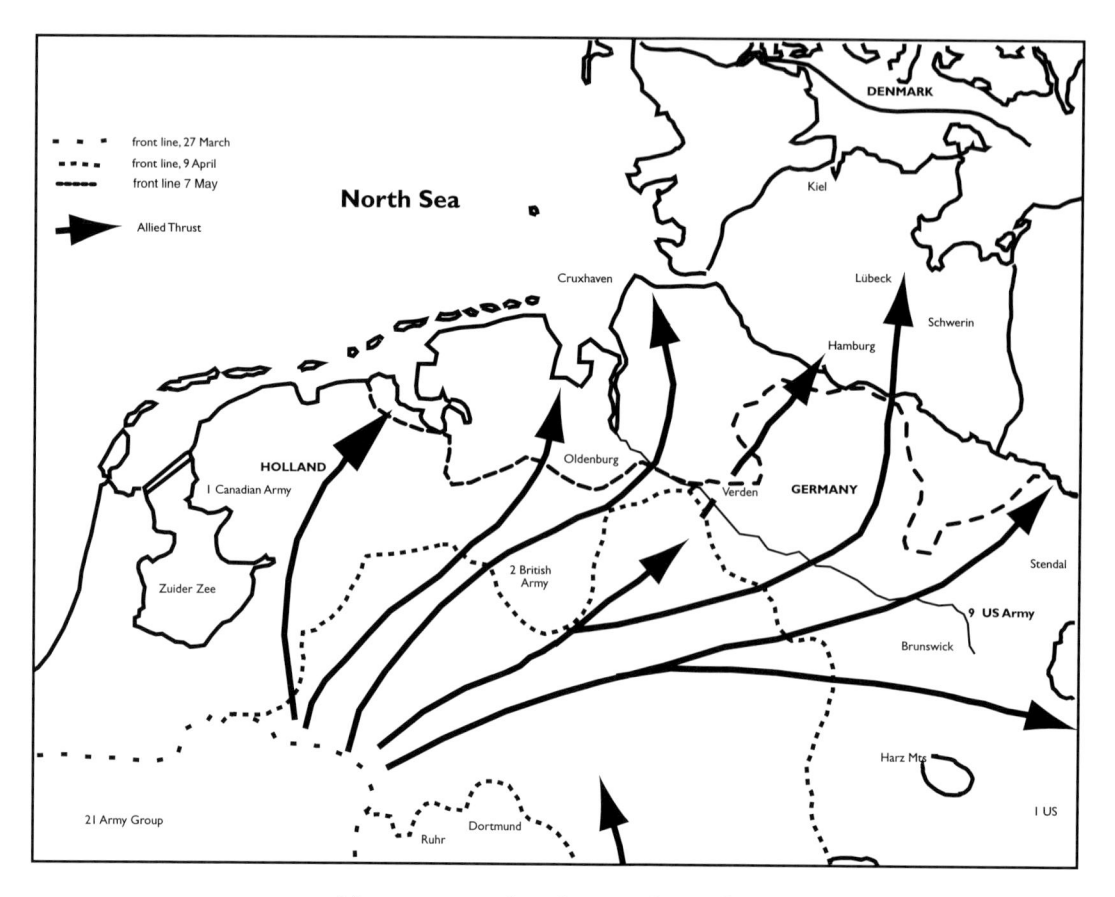

ABOVE: **Montgomery's advance into Germany.**

casualties, although German losses were almost four times as large and 29,000 prisoners were also taken. Meanwhile, however, the US First Army under Bradley's Army Group had unexpectedly captured a bridge across the Rhine at Remagen and Bradley now pressed

Eisenhower for an increased American role beyond the Rhine. Bradley was granted permission to expand the Remagen bridgehead and on 18 March, Eisenhower sanctioned Operation Voyage, an American attack south of the Ruhr, which would now complement rather than support Montgomery's new offensive in the north, code-named Operation Plunder. After three weeks of preparation, this commenced during the early hours of 24 March, when elements of the British Second Army made an amphibious crossing of the Rhine at Wesel. A few hours later, these assault crossings were backed up by the last airborne operation of the war. Both British and American parachute and glider troops were landed on the far bank to secure the high ground and although heavy casualties resulted from being dropped amongst German positions, they had achieved their objectives by the end of the day. Meanwhile, on 25 March, Bradley launched Voyage from the Remagen bridgehead and the newly acquired one at Oppenheim. The chief objective of Plunder and Voyage was the encirclement of the German Army Group B, which was positioned in the Ruhr between the Allied bridgeheads. On 27 March, therefore, Montgomery ordered the US Ninth Army to breakout from the Wesel bridgehead and form one half of a pincer operation to ensnare Army Group B. On 1 April, this was achieved when the US First and Ninth Armies made contact at Lippstadt. The Ruhr pocket was steadily reduced over the next 18 days and a total of 317,000 prisoners were taken, the largest single surrender achieved by the western Allies.

The elimination of Army Group B tore a large hole in the German line and the way to Berlin now lay open. This ultimate prize, for long the cherished target of Montgomery, had, however, already been denied him. On 28 March, Eisenhower changed his overall strategic plan.

Without consulting the British or American governments, he sent a message to the Soviet leader, Stalin, stating that the German capital would be left to the rapidly advancing Red Army and that the western Allies would instead thrust towards Dresden on the River Elbe and no further. Eisenhower's decision was founded both on his desire to avoid any possibility of clashes between his forces and the Red Army and in response to intelligence reports that Hitler was planning a last-ditch stand in the Alps, in the so-called 'National Redoubt'. Churchill was horrified at Eisenhower's decision and demanded that it be reversed, but when the American Joint Chiefs of Staff endorsed Eisenhower's plan, Churchill was obliged to acquiesce, an indication that Britain was by now the junior partner in the alliance. In military terms however, Montgomery was the major loser. Having been led to believe that he would lead the main Allied thrust into Germany and that it would be directed at Berlin,

Montgomery instead received orders to hand the US Ninth Army back to Bradley once the Ruhr pocket had been eradicated and thereafter, protect Bradley's northern flank while the latter made the main thrust towards Dresden. This decision effectively ended the long-running strategic dispute between Montgomery and Eisenhower and handed the final glory to Montgomery's American rivals.

While Bradley's forces raced eastwards into the space formerly occupied by Army Group B – Magdeburg on the Elbe, a mere 75 miles from Berlin, was reached on 11 April – Montgomery dutifully executed his new orders as 21st Army Group began to clear the north German coast with few serious delays. After Bremen fell on 25 April following a bitter battle, the British and Canadian armies moved swiftly towards the Elbe where Hamburg was captured without a fight on 2 May. Simultaneously, in response to Churchill's fears that Denmark might fall into the Soviet sphere, an advance was made beyond the Elbe into Schleswig-Holstein where Lubeck was reached on 2 May and contact made with Soviet troops the following day at Wismar. On 4 May, Montgomery regained a measure of pride and some satisfaction by accepting the first German surrender – of the Netherlands, Denmark and north-western Germany – at his tactical headquarters on Luneburg Heath from Grand Admiral Donitz, the new German head of state following Hitler's suicide on 30 April. With this act, Montgomery's Second World War finally came to an end.

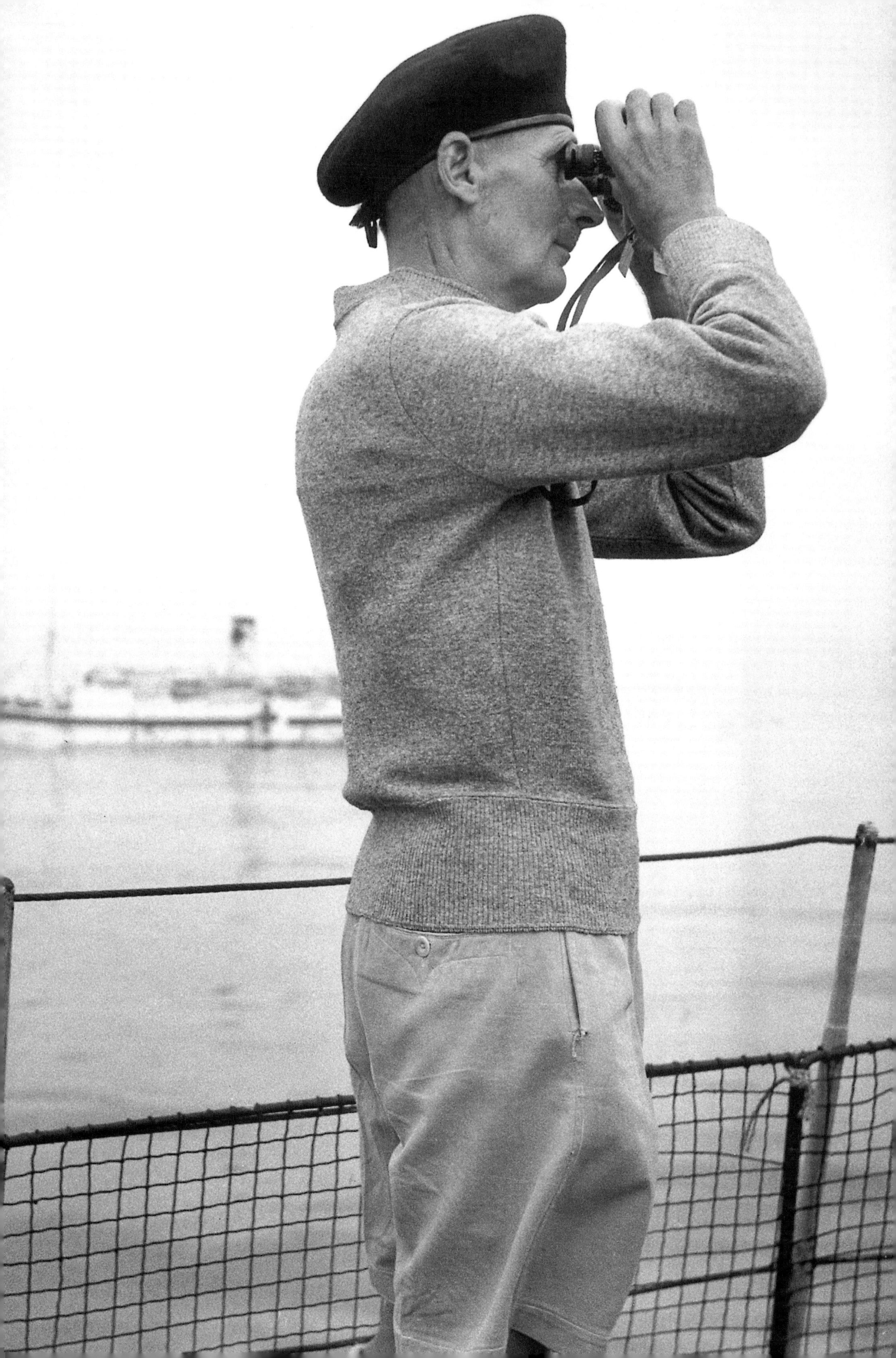

CHAPTER 6

MONTGOMERY AS MILITARY COMMANDER

OVER THE YEARS, Montgomery's reputation as a great military commander has taken a battering. His approach to battle has been described as excessively cautious and unimaginative and over-reliant on sheer brute force to achieve victory. Moreover, the shortcomings in his personality have tended to obscure his undoubtedly significant contribution to Allied victory in the Second World War.

LEFT: **Montgomery observes Allied positions as he approaches the Salerno beachhead, October 1943.**

Montgomery's military technique was distilled from his service in the First World War. His experience at various levels of command of conducting complex all-arms operations, especially during the more fluid final year of the war, had convinced him that, in order to succeed, offensives required meticulous planning and careful control during their execution. The wastefulness of the earlier campaigns on the Somme and at Passchendaele had also instilled in Montgomery a conviction that the lives of the soldiers under his command would not be thrown away in ill-conceived and poorly conducted operations, although he accepted that casualties were necessary to achieve victory.

During the Second World War, these experiences had been moulded by Montgomery into a military method that he liked to describe as a 'colossal crack'. In essence, it was founded on large set-piece battles that involved the concentration of forces, the use of massed firepower from both artillery and, if necessary, aerial bombing, and the proper integration of supporting air power to achieve limited objectives. Such battles were to be conducted according to a painstakingly prepared yet simple blueprint, what Montgomery described as the 'master-plan', the intention of which was to minimize confusion and error in its execution. The more complicated the plan the greater the risk of failure. Before battle could commence, however, Montgomery was insistent that the requisite quantity of forces necessary to achieve victory should be in place beforehand, together with full logistical support. Once battle had been joined, Montgomery sought to maintain the initiative by remaining 'balanced', another of his favourite expressions. This was achieved both by maintaining constant pressure, through a series of different thrust lines, so that the enemy was forced to 'dance to one's tune', and by deploying his forces in such a way that any unexpected enemy action could be immediately countered and success reinforced.

To achieve and maintain this balance and to keep a 'firm grip' on the battle, Montgomery instituted his own distinctive style of command. For instance, in Normandy, Montgomery split his headquarters into three parts, Tactical, Main and Rear, and placed himself during battle at 'Tac HQ', in order to keep himself as close to the fighting troops as possible. To keep himself informed of events on the front line, Montgomery employed liaison officers who travelled forward to determine the situation and a signal service, known as 'Phantom', that eavesdropped on the radio traffic of his own forces. To maintain the tempo of operations, Montgomery was notorious for rarely issuing written orders, preferring instead to communicate his wishes verbally. Indeed, his battle-plans depended upon his subordinate commanders understanding their role in his plan and sticking to it; there was no room for independent initiative. In this respect, Montgomery was particularly adept at selecting professionally competent commanders and staff to serve under him, preferably those he had trained personally, and was ruthless in replacing those who were not up to the task. So long as his senior subordinates followed his wishes, Montgomery allowed them considerable freedom, as personified by Freddie de Guingand, Montgomery's Chief of Staff, who often took decisions on Montgomery's behalf while he was away at the front and was one of the chief unsung heroes behind Montgomery's success.

OVERLEAF: **Montgomery sits for a formal portrait while in Cairo, painted by the official South African war artist, Captain Neville Lewis.**

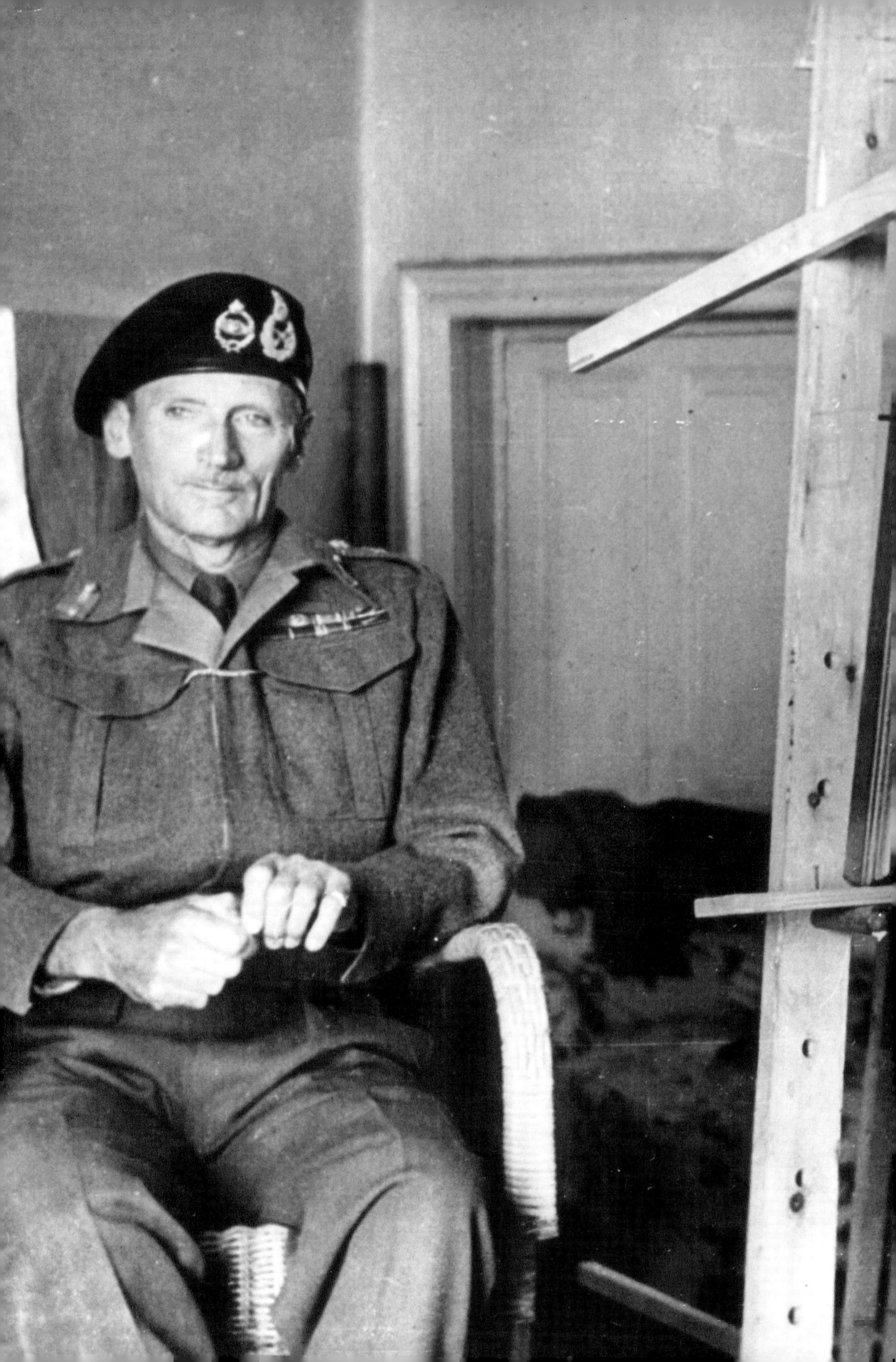

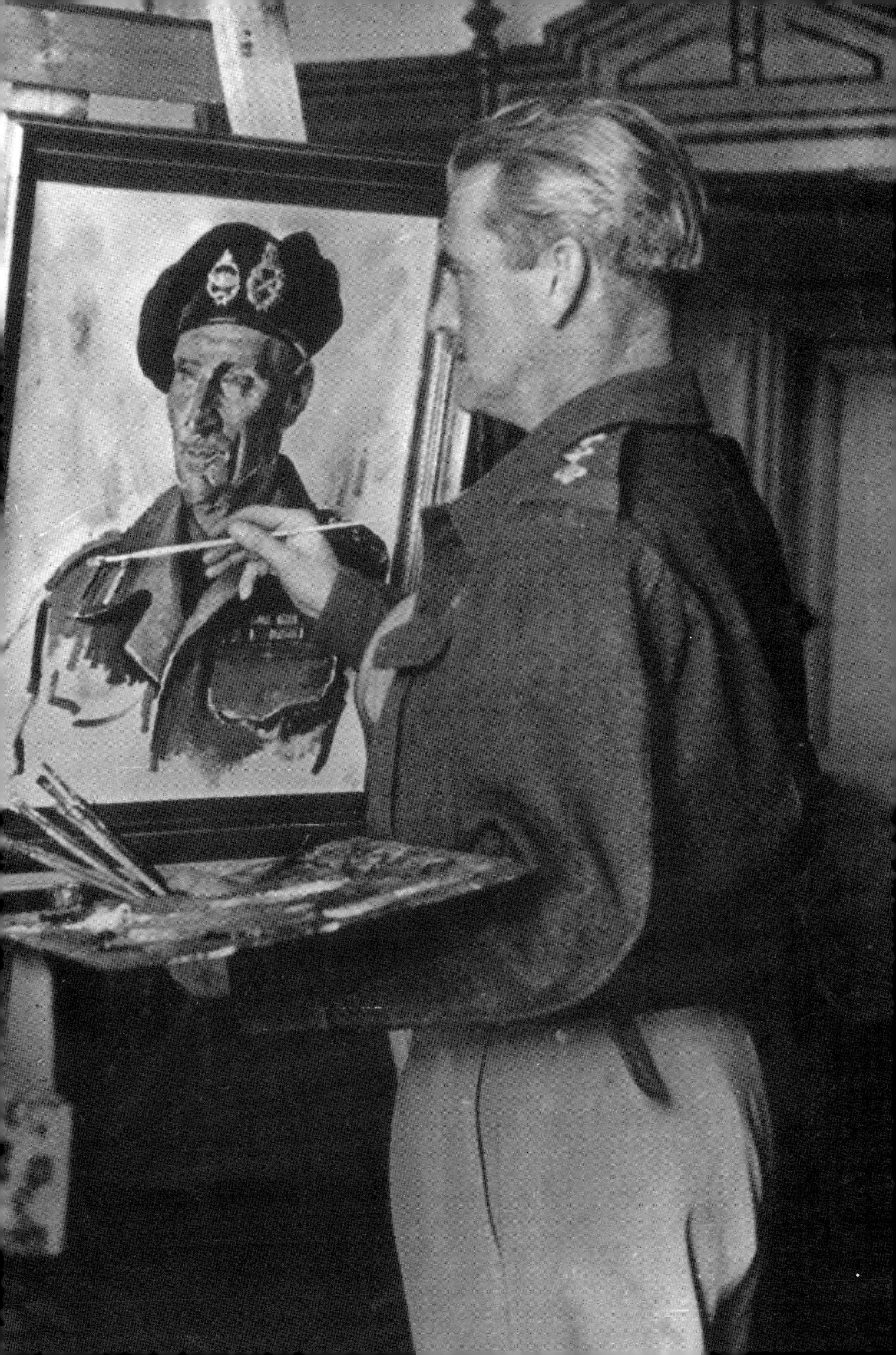

The attritional nature of Montgomery's 'colossal crack' method has often drawn unfavourable comparisons with the great and costly offensives mounted by the British army during the First World War. Montgomery's military art, especially as practiced at El Alamein, certainly appeared to bear the hallmarks of the Somme and Passchendaele – the attritional use of massed firepower at the expense of freedom of manoeuvre – but these resulted chiefly from the lessons and practical necessities of the current war rather than a reversion to the methods of that earlier conflict. The British army's experience in France and, in particular, North Africa, had demonstrated that it was unable to match the Germans in battles of manoeuvre and was better suited to set-piece attrition battles that brought to bear a superiority in firepower and material. Other more practical problems also influenced Montgomery's method. Throughout the second half of the war, the British army was afflicted by an acute manpower shortage and Montgomery's caution and reliance on firepower was often founded upon the need to avoid excessive casualties. This practicality was also fed by Montgomery's desire to avoid a repetition of the slaughter of the last war and the political need to have some measure of the army intact to retain an influence on post-war Europe.

Bound up with Montgomery's emphasis on 'casualty conservation' was the stress he placed on the 'maintenance of morale' in his armies. He was acutely aware of the basic unmilitaristic nature of the men under his command and the necessity of boosting their morale and motivation ahead of battle, not by appealing to their warrior instincts but rather by treating them as workers faced by a particularly unpleasant but vital task. This ability to secure the respect of his troops was central to the transformation Montgomery effected upon the defeated and demoralized Eighth Army ahead of El Alamein. He repeated the dose before D-Day when he set about visiting as many units of the invasion force as possible. Each time, Montgomery would confront an infantryman with the question: 'You. What's your most valuable possession?' The soldier would usually reply that it was his rifle, whereupon Montgomery would counter: 'No, it's not; it's your life, and I'm going to save it for you.' He would then explain how he would never authorize an infantry attack without full artillery and air support. Montgomery's skill in inspiring his troops set him apart from most of his contemporaries as a 'soldier's general' and was a key aspect of his approach to battle.

El Alamein, which established Montgomery's reputation, was the perfect execution of Montgomery's principles, but thereafter, Montgomery was not always consistent in the application of his principles and a number of weaknesses manifested themselves. Not the least of these was his over-caution, particularly in exploiting the breakthroughs created by his 'colossal cracks'. This was evident immediately after El Alamein, when he failed to destroy Rommel's forces during the pursuit towards Tunisia, and his slow progress through the rugged, mountainous terrain of Sicily and Italy caused his critics to remark that he mislaid his genius whenever he met a mountain. Later, in North-West Europe, when Montgomery's usual methods failed to rapidly secure Caen, he was again strongly criticized. Conversely, following his, on this occasion, swift pursuit of the fleeing German forces to Antwerp, Montgomery's reputation was further diminished when his uncharacteristically bold Market Garden plan, which employed a 'single thrust' rather than his 'alternate thrusts' approach, failed at the expense of clearing the strategically important approaches to the Scheldt estuary. Moreover, ironically, Montgomery's desire to limit casualties often saw him call off attacks that met stiff resistance, thereby incurring high casualties for no tangible gain.

RIGHT: **The people of Gabes welcome Montgomery. Girls wearing the colours of the Fighting French rush forward to shake the General's hand, April 1943.**

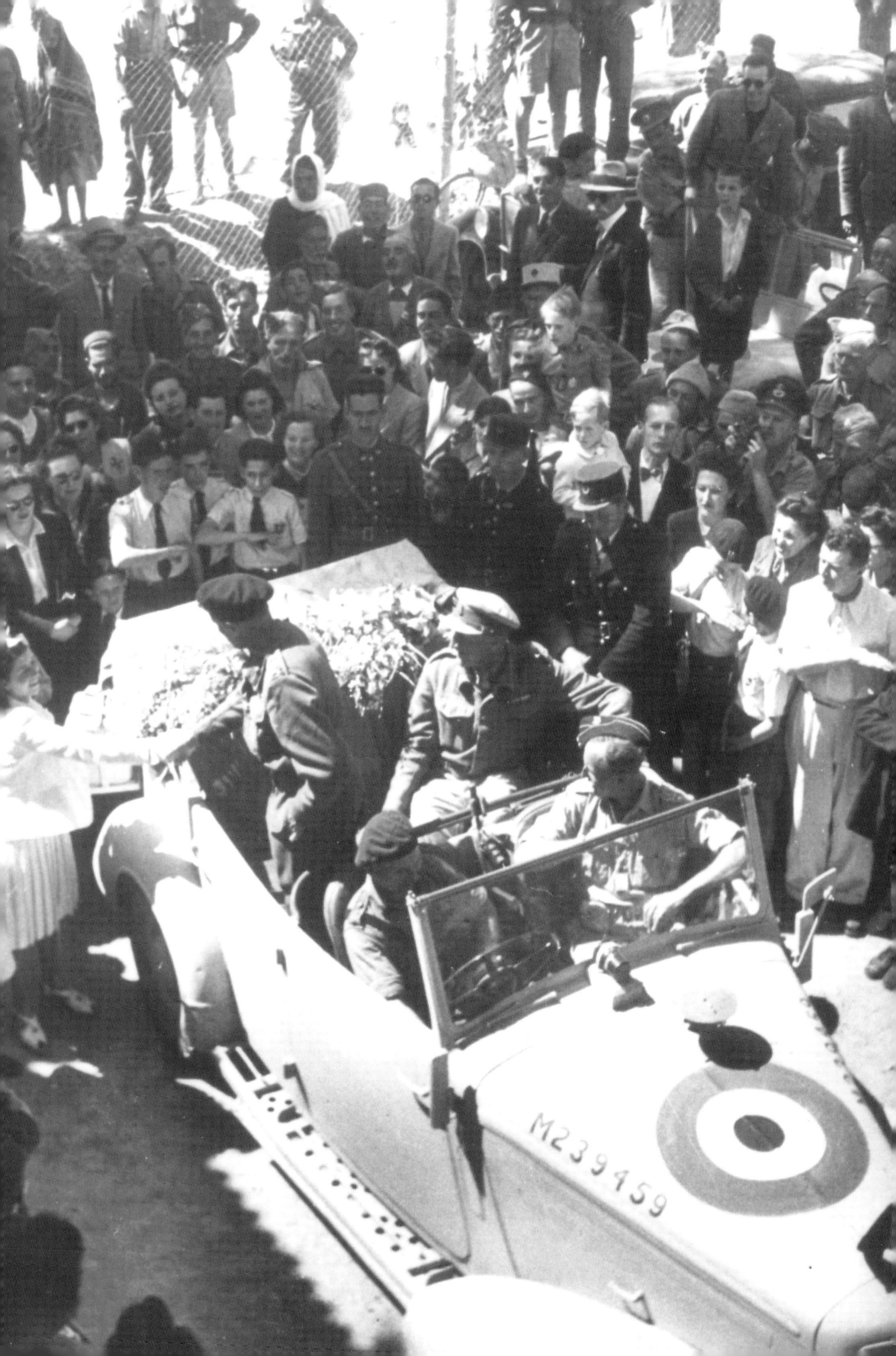
M239459

Nevertheless, these shortcomings cannot obscure Montgomery's very real contributions to the ultimate success of the Allies and the fighting efficiency of the British army. His interventions in the planning for the Sicilian and Normandy landings proved crucial to the success of these operations, while the strategy he pursued in Normandy, of holding the bulk of the German forces in the east around Caen while the Americans effected a breakout to the west, was ultimately vindicated. Montgomery was also instrumental in reviving the fortunes of the British army. Despite its flaws, his battlefield technique succeeded in enhancing the strengths of the British army, while also limiting its shortcomings and the practical restraints within which it had to operate. For his success in transforming his army from its lowest point at the hands of Rommel, to a point where, just two years later, it played a significant role in defeating the undeniably more skilled and efficient German army,

Montgomery can be credited as one of the most competent and inspirational, if not the most gifted, Allied generals of the Second World War.

Whatever the assessments of his contribution to Allied victory and his qualities as a military commander, Montgomery's reputation has, however, been inevitably obscured and tainted by the flaws in his own personality. While he was able to establish a rapport with the ordinary soldier, Montgomery proved incapable of establishing a harmonious working relationship with many of his fellow commanders. His egocentricity, fed by his increasing fame, caused Montgomery to treat many of his contemporaries, particularly the Americans, with barely disguised contempt and an alarming lack of tact, faults that were privately recognised by even his staunchest admirer, Brooke. Moreover, Montgomery's arrogance and conceit, which saw him exaggerate his successes and argue that everything had gone as planned when, such as at Caen, it clearly had not, together with his inability or refusal to co-operate with his American counterparts, especially Eisenhower, threatened to undermine Allied unity on a number of occasions and almost ended his career prematurely. However, it can equally be argued that Montgomery's overweening self-confidence was central to his success as a military commander. This fact was recognised by Churchill himself who, responding to criticism of Montgomery, stated: 'You are jealous; he is better than you are. Ask yourselves these questions. What is a general for? Answer: to win battles. Did he win them without much slaughter? Yes. So what are you grumbling about?'

RIGHT: **This photograph was originally captioned: 'A famous hat and its owner – the Eighth Army Commander Lieutenant-General Montgomery wearing his famous hat for which he is still collecting badges.'**

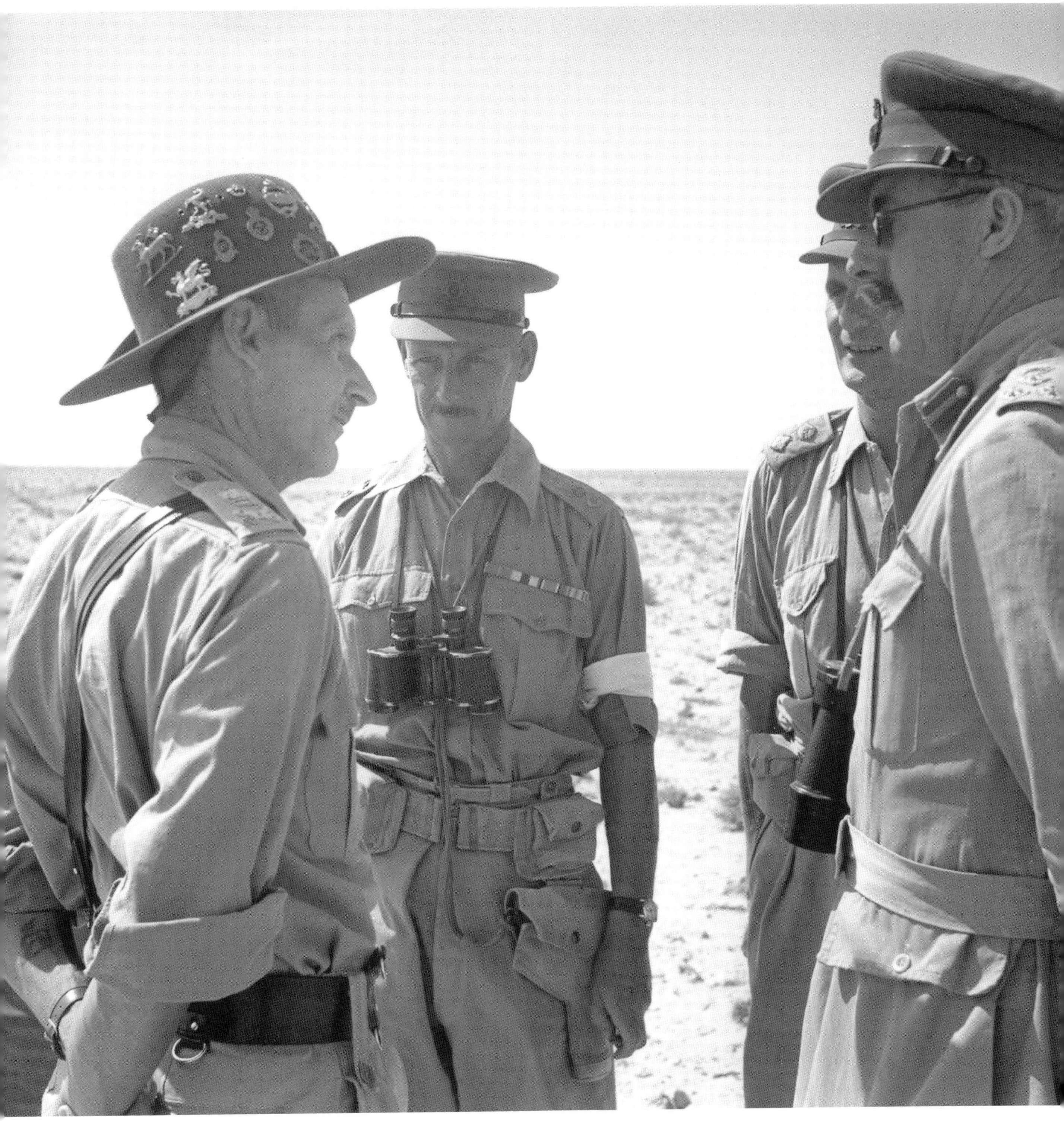

FURTHER READING

Stephen Brooks (ed.): *Montgomery and the Eighth Army: A Selection from the Diaries, Correspondence and other Papers of Field Marshal The Viscount Montgomery of Alamein, August 1942 to December 1943* (London, 1991)

Michael Carver: *El Alamein* (London, 1962)

Alun Chalfont: *Montgomery of Alamein* (London, 1976)

Major General Sir Francis de Guingand: *Operation Victory* (London, 1946)
_____ *From Brass Hats to Bowler Hats* (South Pomfret, VT, 1979)

Carlo D'Este: *Decision in Normandy* (New York, 1983)
_____ *Bitter Victory: The Battle for Sicily, July-August 1943* (London, 1988)

Dominick Graham and Shelford Bidwell: *Tug of War: The Battle for Italy, 1943-45* (London, 1986)

Nigel Hamilton: *Monty: The Making of a General, 1887-1942* (London, 1981)
_____ *Monty: Master of the Battlefield, 1942-1944* (London, 1983)
_____ *Monty: The Field Marshal, 1944-1976* (London, 1986)
_____ *Monty: The Battles of Field Marshal Bernard Montgomery* (London, 1994)

Stephen Hart: 'Montgomery, Morale, Casualty Conservation and 'Colossal Cracks': 21st Army Group's Operational Technique in North-West Europe, 1944-45', in Brian Holden Reid (ed.): *Military Power: Land Warfare in Theory and Practice* (London, 1997)

Alistair Horne and David Montgomery: *Monty: The Lonely Leader, 1944-45* (London, 1994)

Richard Lamb: *Montgomery in Europe, 1943-45: Success or Failure* (London, 1983)

Ronald Lewin: *Montgomery as Military Commander* (London, 1971)

Martin Middlebrook: *Arnhem 1944: The Airborne Battle* (London, 1994)

Field Marshal Sir Bernard Law Montgomery: *Normandy to the Baltic* (London, 1946)
_____ *El Alamein to the River Sangro* (London, 1948)
_____ *Memoirs* (London, 1958)

Brian Montgomery: *Monty: A Life in Photographs* (Poole, 1985)

Alan Moorehead: *Montgomery* (London, 1946)

Cornelius Ryan: *A Bridge Too Far* (London, 1974)

Donald Sommerville: *Monty: A Biography of Field Marshal Montgomery* (New York, 1992)

John Strawson: *El Alamein: Desert Victory* (London, 1981)

Reginald W. Thompson: *The Montgomery Legend* (London, 1967)
_____ *Montgomery the Field Marshal* (London, 1969)

PHOTOGRAPHIC ACKNOWLEDGMENTS

Imperial War Museum: Archives Page 10: q112044, Page 16: q11428, Page 22: h 20268, Page 26: NA 2097, Page 38: e20606 Page 46 e 20020, Page 52: NA 2368, Page 58: E25553, Page 62: E19129, Page 64: E18981, Page 69: E21583 Page 72: NA6114, Page 74: NA 6138, Page 78: N48535, Page 82 NA 4418, Page 86 NA9196, Page 90: NA4381, Page 96: NA9858, Page 100: NA5142 Page 100: NA5142, Page 102: BU2902, Page 105: B5484, Page 108: B15167, Page 114: B5359, Page 118: EA33215, Page 124: BU3417, Page 126: BU3417, Page 128: BU4295, Page 152: BU2912, Page 158: H35663, Page 164: NA 7107, Page 172: BM22317, Page 176: BNA1666, Page 182: E17685. All other photographic acknowledgments: US National Archives and Illustrated London News.

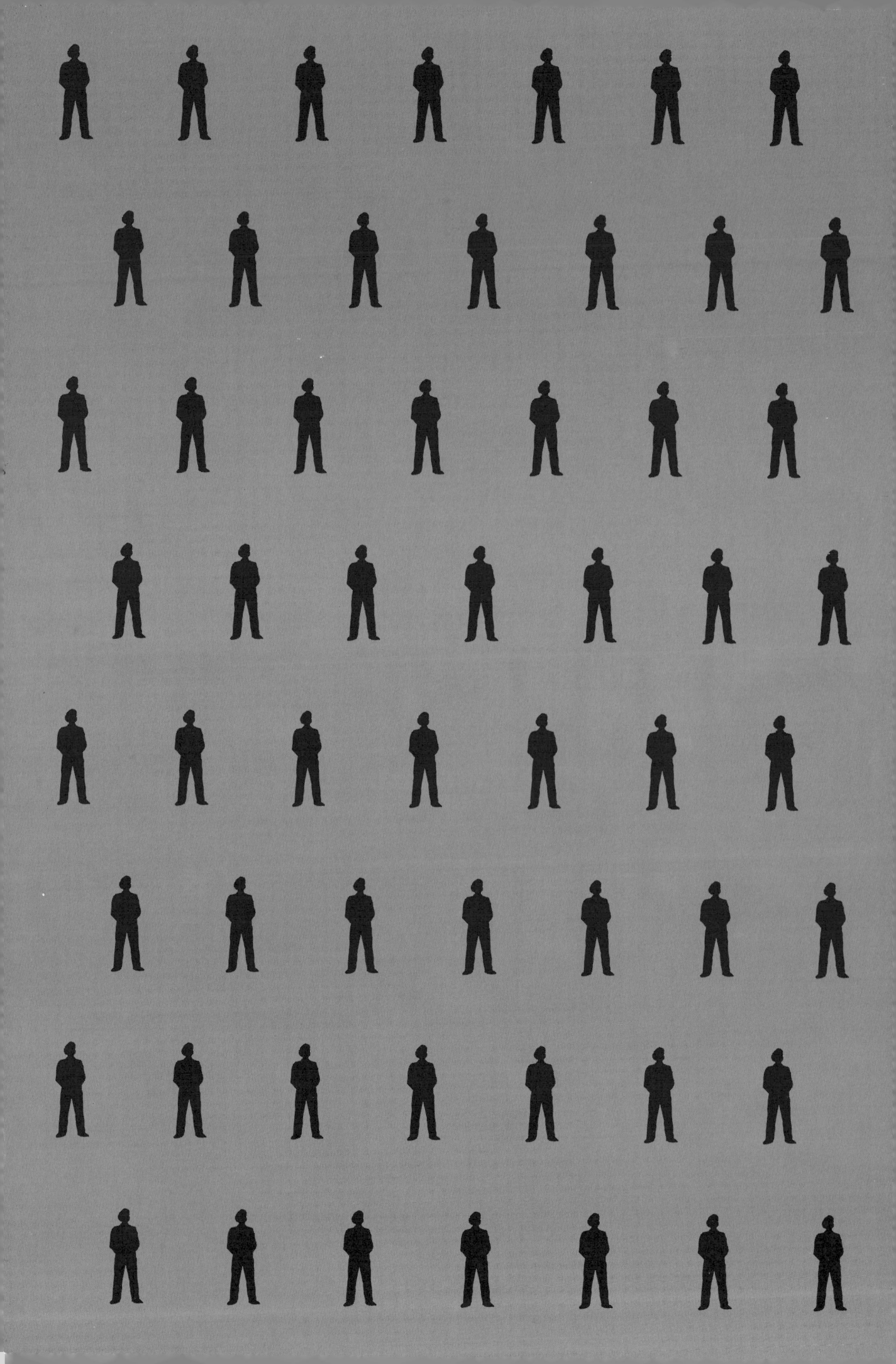